PASS Cambridge BEC Higher

Student's Book

Summertown
Publishing

Published by
Summertown Publishing

29 Grove Street
Summertown
Oxford
OX2 7JT
United Kingdom
www.summertown.co.uk

ISBN 1-902741-35-8

Editor: Anne Williams
Authors: Ian Wood, Louise Pile

Revised Edition Author: Catrin Lloyd-Jones

Series Editor: Elizabeth Clifton

Produced for Summertown Publishing by the Linguarama Group Pedagogical Unit.

Acknowledgements

The publishers would like to thank the following companies for their kind permission to reproduce photographs and other copyright material. They are particularly grateful to the individuals named below for their contribution to the units.

Adidas: Simon White, Brand Communications Manager • Adrian Furnham, University College London • America Online, AOL and the AOL logo are registered trademarks of America Online, Inc. in the United States and other countries. The AOL logo is used with permission • Andrew Eames, journalist • antiphon: Guy Kirkwood • Apple Computer UK Ltd. Apple and the Apple Logo are trademarks of Apple Computer, Inc. registered in the United States and other countries and used with permission • AstraZeneca: Steve Brown, Public Affairs • Belbin Associates: Barrie Watson • BMW AG: Dr Pohlman • British Airways Plc: Jan Dunn, Change Management Consultant, Waterside • British Telecommunications: Neil McLocklin, Workstyle Consultancy Group • British Trade International: Stephen Cornell, China Markets Unit • DaimlerChrysler: Iain Larkins, Legal Executive • Earls Court Exhibition Centre: Jon Allen, Marketing Executive • The Financial Times • Ford Motor Company: Anne-Marie Chatterton, Ford Corporate News • IBM UK: Katie de Cozar, Press Office and Andrew Goldman, UK Communications Manager • IKEA UK: Göran Nilsson, Managing Director • KPMG: Tim Roberts, Director of Media Relations • L'Oréal: Corporate Communications Department • McDonalds: Mina Parmar, Corporate Communications Department • Nestlé: Laura Steel, Advertising Production Executive • www.taps.com: Ian Powell • Top Drawer: Isobel Dennis, Sales Manager • Vodafone AirTouch: Mike Caldwell, Corporate Communications Director.

Printed in Spain by Edelvives

Introduction

The Cambridge BEC examination

The **Cambridge Business English Certificate (BEC)** is an international business English examination which offers a language qualification for learners who use, or will need to use, English for their work. It is available at three levels:

Cambridge BEC Higher

Cambridge BEC Vantage

Cambridge BEC Preliminary

Cambridge BEC Higher is a practical examination that focuses on English in business-related situations. The major emphasis is on the development of language skills for work: reading, writing, listening and speaking.

Pass Cambridge BEC Higher

The book contains:

• Introduction	An introductory unit which gives you information about the examination and this preparation course.
• Core units	Eight double units which cover a wide range of business-related topics. Many of the exercise types are the same as those in the examination.
• Self-study	A section following every double unit to provide consolidation of the language of the units and some examination-related tasks. It also contains a focus on a particular grammatical area to enable you to review your grammar systematically.
• Exam practice	Examination-style exercises following every double unit to provide further practice in the examination skills you will need.
• Exam focus	A section in the centre of the book to prepare you directly for the examination.
• Tapescripts	The content of the audio cd.
• Answer key	Answers to **Self-study** and **Exam practice**.
• Essential vocabulary	A list of the key vocabulary in each unit. **Multilingual key vocabulary lists are available on our website at www.summertown.co.uk**

Language development in *Pass Cambridge BEC Higher*

- **Reading**

  Reading is the most tested skill in the examination. The book therefore contains a lot of reading practice, using authentic, semi-authentic and examination-style texts. Do not panic if you do not understand every word of a text; sometimes you only need to understand the general idea or one particular part. However, you need to read very carefully when answering examination questions; sometimes the most obvious answer on the first reading is not correct and you will change your mind if you re-read the text.

- **Writing**

  In the examination you have to write letters and reports and also describe trends. You need to ensure that you fulfil the task while observing the word limit. If you have good spoken English, it does not necessarily mean that you can write well; to be successful, you need training and practice.

- **Listening**

  Listening is also a very important skill for the examination and most units contain listening activities. You can find the **Tapescripts** to the audio cd at the back of the book. In the Student Book, the tapescripts from the **Exam focus** are shown in blue.

- **Speaking**

  You can find help on how to prepare for the Speaking Test in the **Exam focus** section. In addition, there are speaking activities in every unit.

- **Vocabulary**

  Although vocabulary is tested explicitly only in Reading Test Part Four, it is very important throughout the examination. Many exercises in the **Self-study** sections recycle vocabulary from the units.

- **Grammar**

  A grammatical point is covered in most units. Moreover, grammar is systematically reviewed in the **Self-study** sections of the book. However, the review is brief and you may need to supplement the material.

- **Optional tasks**

  At the end of most units there is an optional task for you to do between lessons, the aim of which is to integrate your studies with real-world activities. For example, you may be asked to visit a company's website and write a report on your findings.

Examination preparation in *Pass Cambridge BEC Higher*

- **Introduction**

  The **Introduction** presents the content of the examination and important examination dates.

- **Core units and Self-study**

  All units contain at least one examination-style exercise and there are also some examination-related tasks in **Self-study**.

- **Exam practice**

  Each double unit is followed by at least two pages of **Exam practice**, which supplement the examination practice in the core units and **Self-study**. Complete Listening Tests follow Units 4 and 8. By the end of the book, you will have practised every part of the examination several times.

- **Exam focus**

  The **Exam focus** section in the centre of the book gives you information about how to succeed in each part of the examination. The Writing and Speaking Test Assessment Sheets provide a framework for you to evaluate your own writing and speaking skills.

Contents

Language

Skills

	Language	Skills

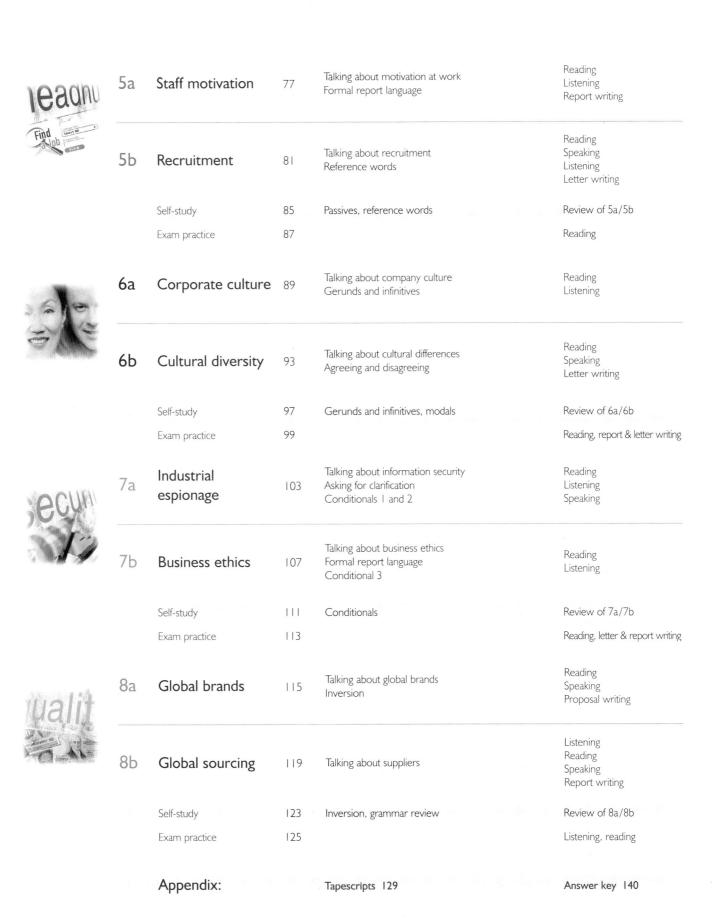

Introduction

Cambridge Business English Certificate Higher

All Cambridge BEC Higher candidates receive a statement of results showing their overall grade (Pass grades A, B, C or Fail grades D, E) and their performance in each of the four papers. Look at the following extract from a sample statement.

Exceptional			
	Reading		
Good			Speaking
		Listening	
Borderline		Writing	
Weak			

Successful candidates receive a certificate showing a single grade. Each paper represents 25% of the total mark.

An overview

The following table gives an overview of the different parts of the examination, how long they take and what they involve.

	Test	Length	Contents
1	Reading	60 minutes	6 parts
2	Writing	70 minutes	2 parts (short description of a graph, formal letter, short report or proposal)
3	Listening	40 minutes	3 parts Approx. 15 minutes of listening material played twice plus time to transfer answers
4	Speaking	16 minutes	3 parts (personal information, short talk and collaborative task) 2 examiners and 2 or 3 candidates

Important Cambridge BEC Higher dates

Your teacher will give you some important dates at the start of your course.
Write these dates in the boxes below.

Cambridge BEC Higher examination

Your teacher will give you the dates of the written papers but can only give you the date
of the Speaking Test after your entry has been confirmed by Cambridge.

- PAPER 1 Reading & Writing Test

- PAPER 2 Listening Test

- Speaking Test (to be confirmed)   Between   and

Entry date

This is the date by which the examination centre must receive your examination entry.

- Entries must be confirmed by

Grades and certificates

Cambridge sends out results approximately seven weeks after the examination.
Successful candidates receive their certificates about four weeks after that.

- Results should be available by

Preparing for Cambridge BEC Higher

1 Look at the following activities which you are going to do on your BEC Higher course. Which two are you most confident about? Which two are you least confident about? Why?

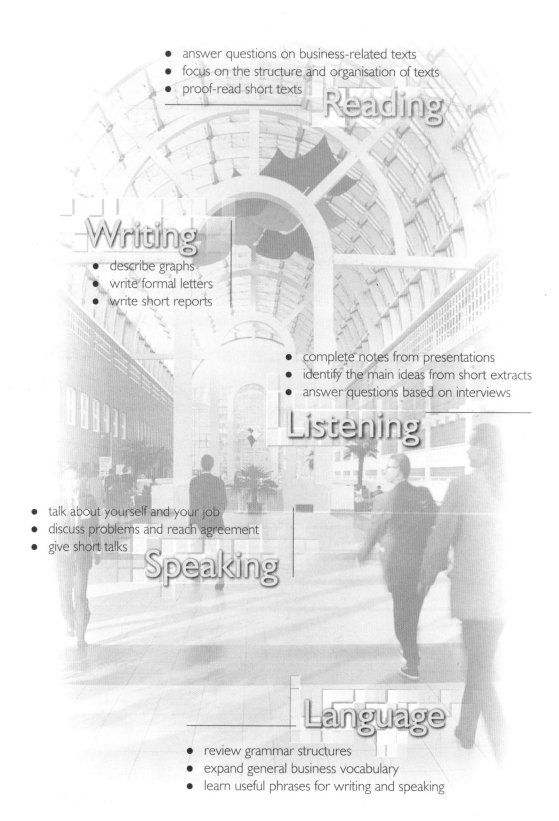

- answer questions on business-related texts
- focus on the structure and organisation of texts
- proof-read short texts

Reading

Writing

- describe graphs
- write formal letters
- write short reports

- complete notes from presentations
- identify the main ideas from short extracts
- answer questions based on interviews

Listening

- talk about yourself and your job
- discuss problems and reach agreement
- give short talks

Speaking

Language

- review grammar structures
- expand general business vocabulary
- learn useful phrases for writing and speaking

2 Which of these are useful for your current job or may be useful in the future?

Quiz: Pass Cambridge BEC Higher

❶ Where would you find the following in this book? Write the unit or page numbers.

1 Information from a famous furniture retailer
2 A list of the top ten global brands
3 An exercise on articles
4 A tapescript of a presentation by a headhunter
5 Advice on writing reports
6 An exercise about linking words and phrases
7 A questionnaire about working from home
8 Advice on the language of agreeing and disagreeing
9 Helpful tips for each of the **Cambridge BEC Higher** papers
10 A card exercise focusing on the language of trends
11 A **Self-study** vocabulary exercise on mergers
12 A checklist to help you evaluate your writing

Helping yourself succeed

❶ Look at the areas below. Add further ideas for using your time outside lessons to help you improve your English skills. How could each activity help you in the exam?

Reading

Reading English language newspapers

Writing

Listening

Speaking

Speaking to my foreign colleagues in English

Language

Work roles

eedbac

Describing work roles

Speaking ❶ Work in pairs. Find out the following information about your partner.

- position
- responsibilities
- duties

Reading 1 ❷ Read the brochure extract on the opposite page from the management consultancy Belbin Associates. How does the WorkSet system use colour to clarify work roles?

❸ Look at the following pie charts and the WorkSet extract. How does the manager's brief compare with what the employee actually does?

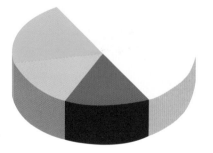

Manager's brief to the employee

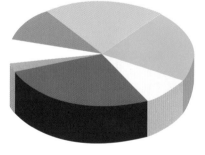

Employee's feedback on the job

❹ A manager assigns the following tasks to different workers. Match each verb with one of the four core WorkSet colours.

yellow (white)	green orange	blue	(white)/yellow	orange
schedule	support	operate	design	co-operate
assist	participate	comply?	decide	follow
green/orange	(pink)orange	blue	yellow	blue

Think of another verb for each core colour.

blue	produce	grey	
yellow	control	white	
green	teach	pink	listen
orange	consult		

What is WorkSet?

WorkSet is an advanced means of setting up jobs and developing employees in response to the changing nature of work. By adopting the use of colours, companies can specify the exact level of responsibility to be allocated to the key tasks that form an employee's job description. WorkSet replaces the often static job description with a more dynamic short-term job brief.

The employee interprets the manager's brief and uses it as a framework for approaching the tasks that make up the job. A feedback and review process then enables the manager to keep abreast of what the employee actually does and provides an opportunity to jointly assess performance, re-align the job and decide on the development needs of the employee.

Core colours

 BLUE WORK refers to tasks an employee has to carry out in a prescribed way to an approved standard. Example: machining an engineering component to a specification.

involves personal responsibility for meeting an objective. Exactly how the work is done does not matter too much as long as the goal is achieved. Example: initiating procedures to reduce costs by 15%.

 GREEN WORK refers to tasks that vary according to the reactions and needs of others. Example: helping the hotel service manager at times of peak occupancy.

 ORANGE WORK involves shared rather than individual responsibility for achieving an objective. Example: contributing to a management team.

Employee feedback colours

 GREY WORK refers to work which is incidental to the job and involves responding to situational needs. Example: being asked to entertain a visitor.

 WHITE WORK refers to any new or creative undertakings outside the employee's formal duties which may lead to improvements. Example: revising standard customer service letters.

PINK WORK demands the presence of the employee but serves no useful purpose. Example: attending meetings where nothing new is learnt and no contribution to decision-making is encouraged.

Listening **5** Five people talk about their jobs. Listen and decide which improvement each speaker would most like to see.

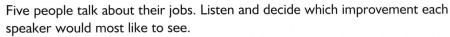

1 ...B	A more responsibility
2 ...D	B more teamwork
3 ...B	C fewer routine tasks
4 ...E	D more flexible hours
5 ...A	E fewer interruptions
	F clearer objectives
	G more creative work
	H more managerial support

Language **6** Look at the present simple and present continuous forms in the following sentences. Find further examples of these forms in the tapescript and discuss how they are used.

*I **work** for the UK subsidiary of a Japanese company.*
*I'**m working** for a small leisure group on a one-year contract.*

Speaking **7** Work in pairs. Use WorkSet to produce a pie chart describing your partner's job.

Report writing

Reading 2 **1** Barrie Watson of Belbin Associates has just led a Team Leadership Workshop at Ekstrom Engineering. Read his report on the workshop. How did he use WorkSet?

BELBIN

Report on Effective Team Leadership Workshop

The aim of this report is to summarise issues arising from the recent Team Leadership Workshop at Ekstrom and recommend appropriate action.

Findings

The workshop began with an assessment of how the Ekstrom team leaders understood their roles. Perceptions ranged from assigning and checking other people's work to motivating others to do the work. This disparity clearly showed that the team leaders had different understandings of their roles and that Ekstrom therefore needed to communicate its expectations more explicitly.

In order to do this, Ekstrom identified key tasks and used WorkSet colours to illustrate the precise level of responsibility which could be allocated to each. A task such as communicating with the team, for example, might be approached in a variety of ways:

- I give my staff instructions every morning. (Blue work)
- I let my staff decide on the best approach for themselves. (Yellow work)
- My team and I discuss how to do each job. (Orange work)

Having identified the different possible approaches to each key task, the company was able to select which was most appropriate and communicate its expectations in terms of the skills and behaviour required.

Conclusions

It is clear that Ekstrom needs to ensure that its team leaders are capable of performing key tasks in a manner compatible with company expectations. However, whilst the appropriate skills can be developed through in-company training, changing behavioural attributes is much more difficult.

Recommendations

We strongly recommend, therefore, that Ekstrom sets up assessment centres where existing team leaders and new applicants can be screened to ensure that they have the appropriate attributes for effective team leadership.

Barrie Watson
Belbin Associates, February 2000

3-4 Bennell Court, Comberton, Cambridge CB3 7DS,
Telephone: 01223 264975, Facsimile: 01223 264976, e-mail: belbin@belbin.com

2 Read the report again and answer the following questions.

1 What were the team leaders asked to do first?
2 What did this show?
3 What did the use of WorkSet colours then allow the company to do?
4 Why does Barrie Watson distinguish between skills and attributes?
5 How can Ekstrom ensure its team leaders have the right attributes?

BelBin
WorkSet
Adding Colour and Clarity to Jobs

3 Complete the following information with phrases from the report.

Report writing

The following phrases are useful when writing reports.

● **Introduction**
This report aims/sets out to ...
summarise issues arising from the recent Team Leadership Workshop at Ekstrom and recommend appropriate action.

● **Findings**
It was found that ...
perceptions of leadership's roles are seen very differently.

● **Conclusions**
It was decided/agreed/felt that ...
Ekstrom needs to ensure that its team leaders are capable of performing key tasks as expected

● **Recommendations**
It is suggested that ...
Ekstrom sets up an assessment centre for screenings to ensure every employee has the appropriate attributes

Writing **4** Use WorkSet colours to compare your job brief with how you actually spend your time at work. Write a 200-250 word report describing your findings and recommending any necessary changes. Consider the following.

● the title of the report
● the heading and content of each paragraph
● useful phrases for each paragraph

homework !

Company structure

Types of company structure

Speaking **1** Look at the following diagrams. What kind of company structure do you think each one represents?

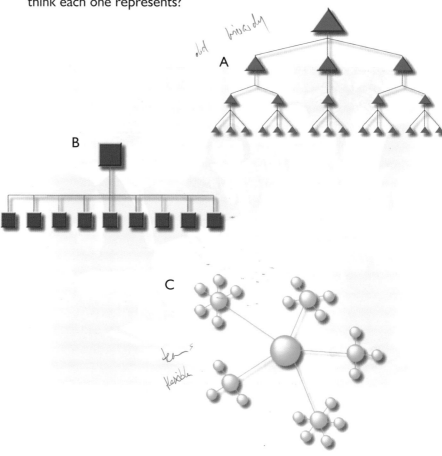

Reading **2** Read the article on the opposite page. What are the advantages and disadvantages of each company structure?

3 Read the article again and answer the following questions.

1 What is the difference between operating and management processes?
2 How do hierarchical companies ensure control of operating systems?
3 How can entrepreneurial companies be responsive and retain control?
4 Why does information alone not guarantee effective management?

Time for the big small company

*With speed increasingly seen as the key to competitive advantage, the dream is to marry the control of an established company with the responsiveness of a start-up. As **Lynda Applegate** reports, advances in IT now mean that the 'big small' company is finally feasible.*

In the hierarchical companies of the 1960s and 1970s, information moved slowly and channels of communication were limited. Over the past few years, however, large companies have come under ever-increasing pressure to collect, process and distribute information more quickly in order to compete with smaller, more nimble rivals. The key challenge facing any sizeable organisation today is how to achieve responsiveness without losing the control inherent in a hierarchical structure.

All types of organisation are controlled through two sets of processes. Operating processes define how a company produces, sells, distributes and supports its products and services. Management processes define how a company directs, co-ordinates and controls these operations. Typical management processes include planning, budgeting and human resource management.

Traditional hierarchical organisations control operating processes through standardisation of jobs. These jobs are separated into sequential steps and carried out under direct supervision. However, the line workers lack both the authority and motivation to improve these routine tasks and are limited by their local view of the business. Management processes in such companies are also hampered by the time it takes to recognise that change is needed. Thus, hierarchical control is only truly effective in relatively stable business environments where change happens slowly.

Entrepreneurial organisations, on the other hand, allow fast response without any loss of control. Daily personal interaction between the owner and employees ensures flexibility and responsiveness, while instant feedback ensures effective control. However, as the company becomes larger and more complex, this control breaks down and more structured operating and management processes are required.

Information age organisations can manage the complexity of the large hierarchical structure without losing the speed of the entrepreneurial start-up. IT plays a critical role. It co-ordinates complex fast-cycle operating processes and, more importantly, gives decision-makers quick access to detailed, real-time information about operations and market performance. Once all this information is flowing, employees can quickly evaluate their decisions and continually refine both strategy and operations. Organisational control then becomes a dynamic, information-enabled learning process rather than a static monitoring system.

However, although IT makes the 'big small' company possible, it cannot motivate people to use information in order to act on behalf of the organisation. The challenge for organisations is therefore to ensure that managers and employees share the same perspective on the business and are motivated to accomplish the same goals.

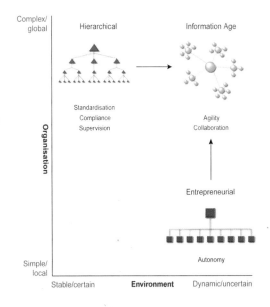

*Adapted from the **Financial Times**, 1 March 1999*

Speaking ❹ Which of the structures is most like the organisation you work for?

Flexible working

Listening ❶ Neil McLocklin from the Workstyle Consultancy Group at British Telecommunications (BT) talks about new working practices. Listen and explain what Options 2000 is.

❷ Listen again and choose one letter for the correct answer.

1 What is the main reason for introducing Options 2000?
   A to reduce the company's operating costs ✓
   B to offer employees alternative work styles
   C to develop the company's technology ✓

2 How has BT's company structure changed?
   A Employees now work in task-based teams.   *purpose*
   B It has now been fully departmentalised.
   C BT is now divided into separate companies.

Neil McLocklin
British Telecommunications
Workstyle Consultancy Group

3 What has been the most important change in BT's company culture?
   ? A The staff have become far more goal-oriented.
   B The employees now demand more varied work.
   C The working atmosphere is more co-operative.   *collaborative*

4 How do staff working from home cope with technology?
   A The company gives them training.   *available ı—*
   B They learn in their own time.
   C The network provides them with help.

5 What has been the impact so far?
   A Productivity has risen.
   B Working hours have increased.
   C The quality of work has improved.

6 What was the hardest part of implementing Options 2000?
   A communicating the general concept
   B co-ordinating flexible workers' hours
   C providing technical back-up and supplies

7 What problems have there been with virtual teams?
   A People did not know how to use e-mail.
   B People sent too much unnecessary e-mail.   *many e-mails !*
   C People resisted using e-mail.

8 How does Neil see the future of offices?
   A He thinks people will stop using them altogether.
   B He thinks they will only be used for meetings.
   C He thinks their role will remain unchanged.

Language ❸ Look at the tenses in the following sentences. Find further examples of these forms in the tapescript and discuss how they are used.

*Surveys **showed** that 96 per cent of our staff **wanted** to work at home.*
*We**'ve had to** develop 24-hour 365-day-a-year support services.*
*We**'ve been developing** a project-oriented culture.*

Speaking ❹ Work in pairs. Use the BT questionnaire to assess the suitability of your partner's job for home-based working. What other factors would be important?

Home-based Working Questionnaire

Please complete the questions and use this document in discussions with your line manager.

Q1 On average, how much time do you currently spend each day commuting?

less than 30 mins	30-60 mins	60-90 mins	90-120 mins	120+ mins

pendeln

S⁻10' x Away

Q2 What percentage of your time is currently spent on the following?

	less than 10%	10-25%	25-50%	50-75%
Travelling on business	✗			
Attending meetings		✗		
Dealing with e-mail		✗		
Dealing with paperwork (hard copy)		✗		
Working on the company network	✗			

Q3 How many times a week do you need to see the following people face-to-face?

	daily	2-3 times	once	less
Your manager		✗		
Your colleagues				✗

Q4 What do you see as the potential benefits to you of home-based working?

I prefer to separate strictly my place of work for any private living spaces,

Writing ❺ Write a 200-250 word report assessing the suitability of your job for home-based working. Separate the report into logical paragraphs with appropriate headings.

Optional task ❻ Visit BT's *Working From Home* website at www.wfh.co.uk. What are the most important practical considerations when setting up your own home office?

1 Choose the correct word to fill each gap.

Research has shown that in today's dynamic working environment the traditional job description is no longer doing its job. Today's jobs are not (1) _static_ - they are constantly changing. This leads to (2) _ambiguity_ with employees uncertain of their precise work roles. This can be illustrated by the following quotation from a job description: 'Meet or exceed customer (3) _expectations_.' The initial reaction may be that this (4) _statement_ is perfectly clear but on closer examination it poses a number of questions. For example, is it (5) _authorising_ employees to do whatever they feel is necessary to (6) _achieve_ this end without restrictions? Or is it saying (7) _follow_ our procedures and this will be the outcome? Who knows? Perhaps the manager, but the description certainly does not (8) _clarify_ things sufficiently from the employee's point of view.

	A		B		C	
1	A	static	B	routine	C	standard
2	A	disparity	B	initiative	C	ambiguity
3	A	undertakings	B	objectives	C	expectations
4	A	schedule	B	feedback	C	statement
5	A	authorising	B	allocating	C	prescribing
6	A	support	B	achieve	C	carry out
7	A	follow	B	comply	C	serve
8	A	highlight	B	identify	C	clarify

2 Use the words to write sentences with *job*.

He re-aligned certain aspects of the job.

carry out

aspects   brief

highlight

communicate   responsibilities

description   (**job**)   classify

feedback   monitor

re-align

set up   enjoy

duties

3 Use the prompts to write sentences to be included in a formal report.

1 'There's a lack of communication in Sales.'
(it/feel) It was felt that there was a lack of communication in Sales.

2 'Let's organise some training for our team leaders.'
(it/suggest) It has been suggested to organise some training ...

3 'We're going to bring in a consultant.'
(it/decide) It has been decided to bring ...

4 'It seems team leaders' roles aren't clear enough.'
(it/find) It was found that team leaders ...

5 'OK, we'll start implementing WorkSet next month.'
(it/agree) It has been agreed to start

6 'Ekstrom needs to set up new assessment centres.'
(we/recommend) We recommend to ...

Present simple and continuous

4 Complete the e-mail. Put each verb in brackets into the correct form of the present simple or continuous.

Sally

Colin (**1** *want*) _wants_ a meeting on Friday morning at 10.30 to discuss ways of improving team leadership within the company. I know we usually (**2** *hold*) _holds_ our weekly sales briefings then but Colin (**3** *say*) _says_ this is more important. He's worried that our team leaders (**4** *not/delegate*) _are not delegating_ anywhere near enough responsibility and that could be the reason why the atmosphere (**5** *not/seem/get*) _seems not getting_ any better around here. Colin must be pretty worried because he (**6** *even/bring*) _is even bringing_ in a consultant. Remember the guy we had in the summer? Well, I (**7** *think*) _think_ it's the same one again, so he should be good. Some of the things he showed us last time about time management were really useful. As a result, I (**8** *definitely/get*) _am definitely getting_ a lot better at prioritising my work nowadays. Anyway, I'd better go.

must rush!

See you on Friday.

Bob

1 Match the words as they appear in the unit.

1 support — intranet
2 virtual — services
3 corporate — manager
4 line — organisation
5 business — support
6 hierarchical — environment
7 on-line — costs
8 operating — team

2 Complete the table.

Verb	Noun	Adjective
standardise	standard	standard
diverse	diversity	divers?
respond	response	responsive
operate	operation	operable
suit	suit	suitable
supervise	supervision	supervised
vary	variation	varied

3 Which word in each group is the odd one out?

1 collaborative (remote) team-based co-operative
2 stable static (sequential) routine
3 responsive dynamic flexible (virtual)
4 separate divide (specify) break down
5 back up resist hamper prevent
6 evaluation feedback interaction assessment
7 accomplish (challenge) manage achieve
8 strategy concept (impact) plan
9 paperwork hard copy e-mail stationery
10 (motivation) authority control supervision

4 Complete each sentence with a suitable preposition.

1 The company is separated _in_ several different business units.

2 People come together _for_ a specific purpose and then go on to join new teams.

3 Some managers worry that staff can only work if they're _under_ direct supervision.

4 I spend most of my day working _on_ the company network.

5 Some people find it hard to cope _with_ working from home.

6 Management should encourage staff to use information _on_ behalf of the organisation.

5 Some of the following lines contain an unnecessary word. Underline any extra words in lines 1-12.

1 Many firms now offer home-based working opportunities
2 to their staff as those demands for more flexible
3 arrangements grow. Companies such like the BBC, for
4 example, are running pilot schemes where managers,
5 journalists, producers and accountants all have work from
6 home. The manager of one project said, 'It is popular with
7 all staff. They are lot happier, use their time more
8 productively and are less stressed. They are saving money
9 by not commuting and can spend themselves more time
10 with their families.' He also mentioned the need for
11 home-based staff and to be able to cope with technology.
12 'Good information technology support is the absolutely
crucial to the success of any home-working scheme.'

Past simple and present perfect

6 Complete the conversation. Put each verb in brackets into the correct form of the past simple, present perfect simple or present perfect continuous.

● Linda, (**1** you/hear) _have you heard_ the news?

▼ What news?

● They (**2** just/promote) _have just promoted_ Sue to Head of European Sales.

▼ Sue? You must be joking! She (**3** not/even/work) _not even worked_ for the company all that long. When (**4** she/join) _did she join us_, about last May? Anyway, who (**5** tell) _told_ you about it?

● Maurice. I (**6** see) _saw_ him yesterday at the International Sales Conference. Yes, apparently Sue (**7** break) _broke_ all kinds of records since she (**8** look) _has been looking_ after the Central European Region.

▼ But I always (**9** think) _thought_ Francesco (**10** be) _was_ in line for that position.

● Well, it seems Sue (**11** make) _has made_ a huge impression on the board and they're worried they might lose her. Maurice says that headhunters (**12** already/call) _have already been calling_ on a pretty regular basis so ...

▼ And what about poor Francesco? How (**13** he/take) _did he take_ the news?

● I don't really know. Maurice (**14** not/mention) _did not mention_ Francesco at all. But I guess he'll be pretty disappointed. He's certainly made no secret of the fact that he wanted the job.

Reading Test Part One

- Look at the sentences below and the profiles of five international executives.
- Who does each sentence refer to?
- For each sentence 1 - 8, mark **one** letter **A**, **B**, **C**, **D** or **E**.
- You will need to use some of the letters more than once.

Example

0 He was once involved in national politics.

A B C D E
■ □ □ □ □

---

1 He has cut operating costs by reducing the number of senior staff. *D*
2 He does not enjoy making presentations and speeches. *C*
3 He started his career working for a television station. *B*
4 He improved the company's financial position by selling off assets. *E*
5 He is expanding the company with a series of takeovers. *A*
6 He is famous for his imagination and tough business strategies. *B*
7 He has been with the same employer all his working life. *E*
8 He has worked in a variety of different industries. *C*

A **Lord Wootten, *Chairman, Unimarket***
Lord Wootten has recently returned to Unimarket, the large retail food chain, after a 20-year absence. Whilst away, he held a variety of posts in the Conservative Party including that of Chief of Staff to the British Prime Minister for six years, where his skills as an effective public speaker won him great respect. He then returned to the industry as one of the two architects behind the dramatic revival of the Remco supermarket chain. His comprehensive and varied experience of the retail food sector will make a huge impact on Unimarket and he has already embarked on an ambitious policy of major acquisitions. *S*

B **Steven Waugh, *Chief Executive Officer, DigiCom***
Steven Waugh, the driving force behind DigiCom for over 25 years, retires this year. Known for his quick decision-making, he is seen as one of the most outspoken and ruthless operators in the world of business. These qualities have often made life difficult for DigiCom competitors, who have regularly been faced with bitter price wars and innovative promotional campaigns, often masterminded by the CEO himself. Born in Queensland, Waugh first cut his teeth on Australia's Channel 9 before entering broadcasting in Britain. Never a great believer in political correctness, he is famous for spending his time aboard his luxury cruiser indulging in gourmet food and champagne.

C **Mark Boucher, *Chairman, Gladstone***
Mark Boucher, 53, chairs Gladstone, the base-metals group recently demerged from Corgen of South Africa and floated in Amsterdam. Since the breakaway, Gladstone's operating profit has grown to $92m, even though experts have described the company as overstaffed and inefficient. Boucher is a reserved man who is reluctant to address large meetings but reveals, when pressed, a dry sense of humour. He has had an unusual career path, including a spell working for the North American Space Agency, followed by a stint running a satellite TV station.

D **Erik Johanssen,** *Chief Executive, MorgenReynolds*

MorgenReynolds' CEO Erik Johanssen admits to crying occasionally and says he is not the tough hard-nosed businessman that people expect when they meet him. He is, however, universally regarded as a shrewd politician within the industry. A self-styled company man, the chain-smoking 55 year-old Johanssen has been with Morgen for over 20 years. Since Morgen took over the innovative but under-performing Reynolds, Johanssen has streamlined the business radically, axing half of Reynolds' top managers. Johanssen lives modestly in Stockholm and travels to work by underground.

E **Joe Anderson,** *Chief Executive, Dayton International Hotels*

Joe Anderson joined the imaginative Seattle-based Foyles restaurant chain after graduating in 1963. He worked his way up through the ranks, performing a variety of different roles, eventually becoming the Managing Director in 1976 and joining the parent company's executive board in 1980. In 1994 he became CEO and President of the group's Dayton International Hotels division. Anderson has focused on Dayton's core restaurant and hotel activities and reduced the group's debts by disposing of several properties and a chain of beauty salons. His next project is likely to be the search for strategic alliances with major European hotel chains.

Reading Test Part Five

- Read the article below about working practices in Europe.
- For each question **1 - 10**, write **one** word.

Example

0 | W | E | L | L | | | | | |

UK workplace becomes more flexible

A recent survey has shown that employers are using increasingly flexible types of employment to meet their changing requirements. There has been a dramatic rise in the use of part-time contracts and flexitime as **(0)** well. as in the number of temporary workers, including seasonal workers and people on fixed-term contracts.

The number of men working part-time in the UK **(1)** more than doubled between 1984 and 1998. Over the same period, the number of women working part-time rose by one million, **(2)** from 4.4m to 5.4m. Flexi-time is now used by 10 per cent of full-time employees, mostly in professional occupations. Shift working is also **(3)** on the increase, with 14 per cent of UK employees now working **(4)** some kind of shift system.

The aim of the survey is to show **(5)** how much employment practices and working patterns have changed in the last 20 years. British workers still work **(6)** the longest hours within Europe, with the average working week for a male full-timer being 46 hours in the UK, compared to 39 hours in Belgium. Women in the UK also work longer hours than **(7)** their European counterparts, with an average week of just over 40 hours.

The role of women in the workplace **(8)** is also changing. There has been an increase in the number of women working in traditionally male areas **(9)** such as management and administration. Almost 33 per cent of women now work in professional, technical or managerial positions, **(10)** up from 29 per cent in 1991. However, secretarial and clerical occupations still remain firmly associated with women.

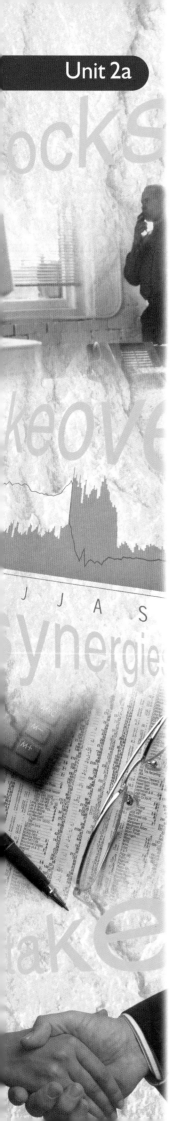

Stocks & shares

Share prices

Speaking ❶ Where can you find out about a company's share price?

Reading ❷ Look at the following extract from the Nasdaq-amex stock market listings. Match the letters a-f with the explanations below.

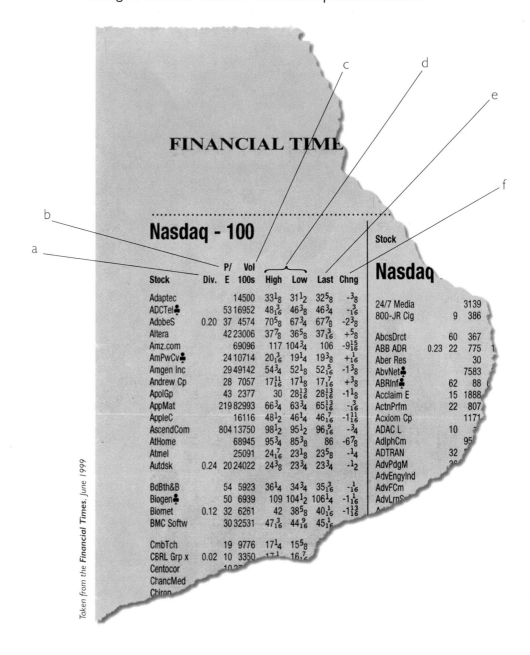

Taken from the Financial Times, June 1999

✓ 1 f change in share price compared with previous day
✓ 2 a amount paid out to shareholders for each dollar invested
✓ 3 e price of shares at close of previous day's business
✓ 4 c number of company's shares traded on previous day
✓ 5 d highest and lowest prices during previous day
✓ 6 b price/earnings ratio (current share price divided by earnings per share)

Speaking **3** How common is investing in shares in your country?

idiological

it gets more + more popular internet - platform e-banking

Market trends

Listening 1 **1** Listen to a television report about the share prices of Internet companies. How have they performed over the last year?

2 Listen again and choose one letter for the correct answer.

1   What drove up the price of Internet shares?
   A   the promise of a quick profit
   B   the lack of availability of the shares *demand exceeded ✓ limited supply*   *demand Nachfrage*
   C   the opportunity of a safe investment   *Supply Angebot*

2   How profitable are most Internet companies?
   A   They now make huge profits.   *long way away*
   B   They just manage to break even.   *not even*
   C   They consistently lose money.

3   Investors are attracted to these companies because
   A   they are expected to make huge profits.   *future revenue / ad spending*
   B   they are such well-known brands.
   C   they are very fashionable at the moment.

4   In order to value these companies, analysts compare
   A   the value of their assets.   *} alternative yardsticks*
   B   the growth in turnover.
   C   the number of customers.   *audiencereach 45% become internet users*

5   The recent collapse in share prices was due to
   A   a sell-off by shareholders.   *of companies*
   B   increased availability of shares.   *flood / saturated market*
   C   over-pricing of shares.

6   The share prices are so volatile because   *trade - online several times a day*
   A   shares are traded at great speed.   *sensitive to news / responsiveness*
   B   the whole Internet sector is still very new.
   C   many companies are new to the market.

7   Katie thinks that share prices will
   A   continue to fall.   *not much more*
   B   make a recovery.
   C   shoot up again.   *don't expect soaring*
   join /fuse

8   As the market develops, Katie believes most Internet companies will
   A   expand through takeovers and mergers.   *as well*
   B   try to enter profitable US markets.
   C   be bought by large established companies.   *Bertelsmann for example*
   Barnes + Noble

Speaking ❸   Would you be prepared to invest in Internet shares? Why/Why not?

No, there is no money to invest

Describing graphs

Speaking ❶   The graph shows the price for Amazon.com shares over a twelve-month period. Your teacher will give you some cards. Describe the graph using all the words on the cards.

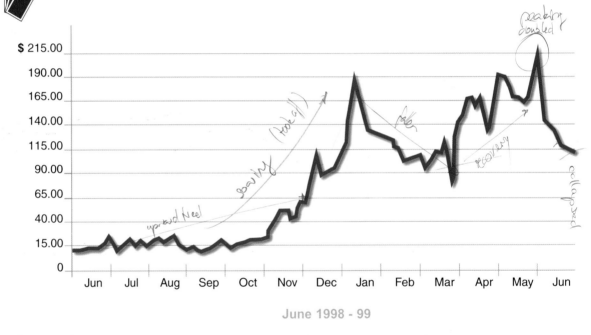

June 1998 - 99

Listening 2 ❷   Now listen to a description of the graph. In what order are the cards used?

Language ❸   Look at the tapescript and find examples of the following.

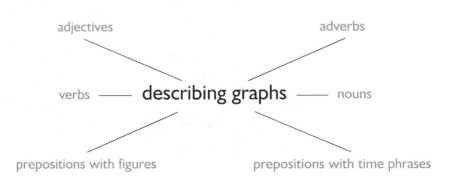

Similarity and difference

The following language is useful when comparing.

- **Similarity**

  Both share prices rose sharply in January.

  Neither company has made a profit yet.

  Like X, Y fell in June.

  X rose *just as* sharply *as* Y.

- **Difference**

  X fell sharply *whereas/while* Y remained steady.

  X fell quickly *compared to* Y.

  Unlike X, Y rose by 10%.

  X rose *far more* dramatically *than* Y.

Writing **4** Look at the share prices of IBM Corporation and America Online, Inc. over a twelve-month period. Write a 120-140 word report comparing the performance of the two shares.

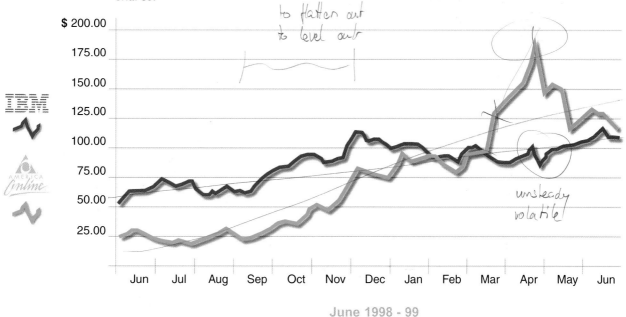

June 1998 - 99

Optional task **5** You have $10,000 to invest in shares. Use the listings in the financial press or on the Internet to buy and sell shares. Check the progress of your investments during your course. Can you make more profit than the interest on a standard savings account?

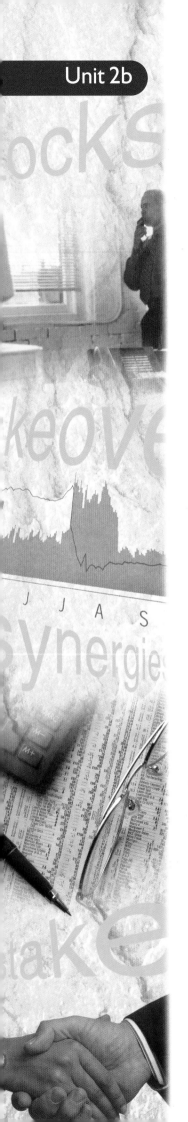

Mergers & acquisitions

(Fusion)

Understanding mergers

agreement

Speaking **1**   Why do companies merge with or acquire other companies? What problems can arise?

4   ★   WORI

in Ma
most ma

UK Trade Secretary clears Coca-Cola Cadbury deal

acquisition

okesman said the
ake an announcement in due course.

Merger talks boost pharmaceutical sector

Helen Arnold reports

The pharmaceuticals industry has been boosted

Commission investigates Airtours bid *= offer* for First Choice

By Joanne Robinson

UK insurer on acquisition trail in Japan

Amid

AlliedSignal and Honeywell set to create global powerhouse

By Tim Longman   *merger*

It was announced today that AlliedSignal and Honeywell are set to

Reading **2**   Read the article on the opposite page about mergers and acquisitions. What benefits and problems are mentioned?

Benefits	Problems
- to remain competitive	- different corporate cultures
- gain access to foreign markets	- different national cultures
- to diversify / new markets	- redundancies
- to grow resources	- different working times
- reduce payroll	
- combining know-how	
- deregulation by one currency only	

1998 was undoubtedly the year of the merger. More companies than ever before joined together in deals that totalled $2.25 trillion and created the world's largest ever bank and the world's biggest oil company. Faced with plummeting oil prices, oil giants Exxon and Mobil sought to achieve economies of scale through a $250bn merger.

There are several factors behind the increase in mergers and acquisitions. Firstly, the accelerated rate of globalisation has left companies desperately seeking overseas acquisitions in order to remain competitive. Deutsche Bank bought its way into the US with its takeover of Bankers Trust, whilst Siemens hopes that its acquisition of Matra, the French defence group, will allow it to gain access to France's railway business, which is dominated by Alstom, the Anglo-French consortium.

Another factor behind the increase in merger activity is the record performance of stock markets, which has enabled companies to finance major acquisitions on the strength of their inflated share prices. Earlier this year Vodafone, the UK mobile telephone operator, acquired its US counterpart AirTouch by making AirTouch shareholders a cash and stock swap offer worth a total of $62bn. The deal created Vodafone AirTouch, the world's largest mobile telecoms group with over 29m customers.

The European banking sector is also seeing a trend towards consolidation, a process accelerated by deregulation, over-capacity and the arrival of the single European currency.

New technology is also making it easier for companies to diversify as different industries come to rely on common technologies. Microsoft, for instance, is busily diversifying into cable and mobile telecommunications as well as WebTV. The US software giant has a $5bn equity stake in AT&T, which recently bought Media One for $57bn. Under the deal, Microsoft will succeed in introducing its recently-launched cable television software into millions of homes in the US and UK.

Not all mergers, however, are the result of global economic trends, political change or technological innovation. BMW's takeover of the Rover Group injected much needed investment into the struggling UK car manufacturer whilst extending BMW's product range. And when the UK pharmaceutical firm Zeneca merged with Swedish drug company Astra, the new company started life with strong combined R&D capabilities, further strengthened by the world's best selling drug Losec in its portfolio of products.

Despite all these potential benefits and their promise of competitive advantage, mergers and acquisitions are not risk-free ventures.

Such alliances are more than just financial agreements; they also involve the coming together of different corporate and, in many cases, national cultures. This can have a destabilising effect on a workforce and may mean projected efficiencies are not delivered. Daimler and Chrysler, for example, face the challenge of integrating two very different corporate and national cultures.

A further destabilising effect is the prospect of redundancies* as companies look to reduce their payroll by restructuring duplicated functions such as marketing and administration. Although shareholders are lured by such short-term savings, there is little evidence to show that mergers and acquisitions actually add long-term value to company performance.

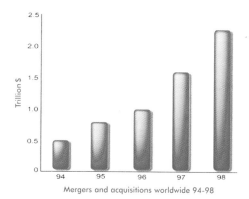

Mergers and acquisitions worldwide 94-98

---

3 Read the article again and choose one letter for the correct answer.

1 Exxon and Mobil merged in order to
  A enter new overseas markets.
  B reduce costs and improve margins.
  C create the world's biggest company.
  D undercut competitors' prices.

2 Vodafone was able to acquire AirTouch by
  A selling highly-valued shares to customers.
  B obtaining a loan based on its share value.
  C exchanging shares as part of the deal.
  D buying under-valued AirTouch shares.

3 What is Microsoft's interest in AT&T's acquisition of Media One?
  A It will raise Microsoft's equity stake in AT&T.
  B It will give Microsoft access to new technologies.
  C It will increase the size of Microsoft's core market.
  D It will help Microsoft break into new markets.

4 Why was the BMW takeover in Rover's interests?
  A Rover was able to raise capital.
  B It extended Rover's product range.
  C Rover gained new distribution channels.
  D It reduced Rover's operating costs.

5 What is the main challenge facing Daimler and Chrysler?
  A Customers may not want to buy foreign products.
  B Workforce reductions could affect delivery times.
  C Their managers might not work together effectively.
  D The cost of the merger will outweigh any savings.

6 Merged companies can usually increase short-term profits by
  A cutting their combined labour costs.
  B boosting the company's productivity.
  C using a single marketing campaign.
  D selling their shares at a high price.

Language ④ Look at the article again and find examples of the following.

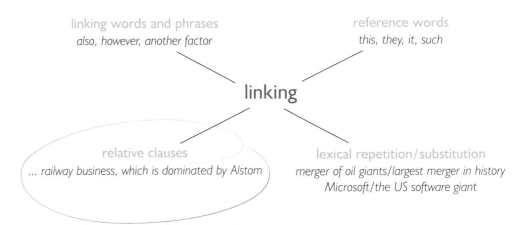

linking words and phrases
also, however, another factor

reference words
this, they, it, such

linking

relative clauses
... railway business, which is dominated by Alstom

lexical repetition/substitution
merger of oil giants/largest merger in history
Microsoft/the US software giant

Speaking ⑤ Think of a recent merger or acquisition. What were the reasons behind it?

A merger of equals

Steve Brown, Media Relations Manager at UK pharmaceutical company Zeneca, addresses shareholders prior to the company's merger with Astra of Sweden. Listen and complete the notes with up to three words or a number.

AstraZeneca news release

Introduction

1 The boards of both Astra and Zeneca have agreed to the terms of an _all-share_ merger of equals to form AstraZeneca.

2 The merger combines two companies with similar _science-based_ cultures and a shared vision of the pharmaceuticals industry.

Merger benefits

3 AstraZeneca will be better able to generate _long-term growth_ and shareholder value.

4 The merged group will benefit from the combined power and _worldwide presence_ of its global sales and marketing resources.

5 Combined sales will rank AstraZeneca as the _third-largest_ pharmaceutical company in the world.

6 Investment in R&D will provide a strong foundation for _innovation-lead_ growth.

7 A $1.9bn R&D budget will make AstraZeneca an attractive partner for _academic institutions_ and biotech companies.

8 Management expects to generate substantial cost improvements through _restructuring_ areas of duplication.

9 Management estimates savings of $1.1bn within the _next 3 years_.

[dinpu?]

10 Staff reductions are expected in areas such as _administration_ and sales.

The Board

11 AstraZeneca will be run by the Chief Executive Tom McKillop and his _executive team_.

12 Percy Barnevik, as non-executive Chairman, will ensure that _strategy and policy_ are regularly reviewed and agreed.

un verbinden wenn adjectiv — a well-known musician
— he is well-known

Your company wants to merge with or acquire another company. Discuss the following.

• which company to merge with or acquire
• the benefits that would result

Visit the www.astrazeneca.com website and write a brief profile of the new company. Include information about its size, products and markets.

① Match the following words with the diagrams.

> recover   general upward trend   peak
>   fluctuate   level off   bottom out

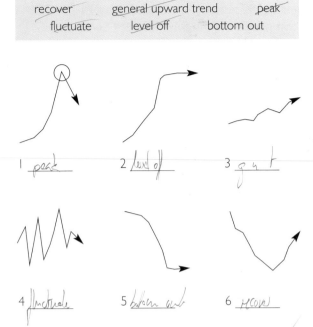

1 _peak_   2 _level off_   3 _g u t_

4 _fluctuate_   5 _bottom out_   6 _recover_

② Complete the text with the following words.

> broker   merger   commission   dividends
> listings   flotation   investment   shares

The first time I ever bought (1) _shares_ was in 1988. It was during the (2) _flotation_ of British Telecom. I didn't really know anything about the stock market but a friend of mine is a (3) _broker_ and he told me BT would be a safe (4) _investment_ . Since then, he's also taught me all about how to read the (5) _listings_ in the financial press. Of course, I pay him some (6) _commission_ but I think he gives me a lot more help than he would a normal client. He'll phone me, for example, if he hears a rumour about a (7) _merger_ or a takeover. He also gives me good information about companies, such as who pays their shareholders the biggest (8) _dividends_ and things like that. His advice doesn't guarantee success, of course, but it's certainly a great help.

③ Do the following statements refer to positive (↑), negative (↓) or neutral (→) trends?

1 We operated at break-even point for most of 1999.
2 Prices really began to take off early this year.
3 The over-supply of shares depressed the markets.
4 Performance of the shares exceeded all expectations.
5 The markets showed investors' lack of confidence.
6 None of the analysts predicted the collapse.
7 Merger rumours caused share prices to shoot up.
8 Prices fluctuated but remained fairly steady overall.

④ Write a 120-140 word report comparing the monthly sales of *Fresh 'n' Cool* with those of the previous year.

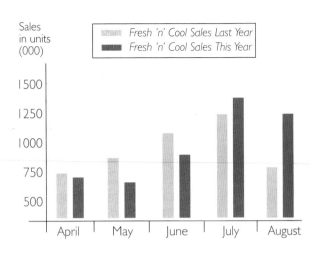

Sales in units (000)

| | Fresh 'n' Cool Sales Last Year |
| | Fresh 'n' Cool Sales This Year |

1500 1250 1000 750 500

April   May   June   July   August

Describing trends

⑤ The graph shows the share price of two companies from 1996 to 2000. Find and correct any mistakes in the text.

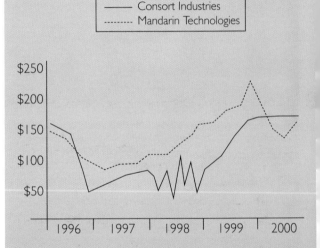

—— Consort Industries
------ Mandarin Technologies

$250 $200 $150 $100 $50

1996   1997   1998   1999   2000

In the start of 1996, shares in Consort Industries stood at $160. However, by the end of the year they have collapsed to just $50. They recovered steady over the next twelve months but have fluctuated sharply all through 1998. In 1999 they continued their recovery climb to $160 per share, where they remained throughout 2000.

Shares in Mandarin Technologies starting trading at $150. Like Consort, Mandarin saw it's shares fall during 1996 and then picked up the following year. This recovery then turns into a general upward trend, what continued until late 1999, when shares peaked at $220. They then collapsed before rise briefly to just over $150 at the end of 2000.

1 Read the article on page 22 again and put the following companies in the correct groups.

AirTouch	Astra	AT&T	Bankers Trust
BMW	Chrysler	Daimler	Deutsche Bank
Exxon	Matra	Media One	Mobil
Rover	Siemens	Vodafone	Zeneca

Acquired another company	Merged with another company	Was acquired by another company
		AirTouch

Now find examples in the article of *the + noun + of*. What nouns follow the phrases? Think of two other nouns to follow each phrase.

the prospect of	redundancies
	expansion
	competition

2 Complete the sentences with the correct form of the following words.

| grow | restructure | merge | takeover |
| benefit | compete | streamline | acquire |

1 The telecoms sector was rocked when Vodafone launched a hostile _takeover_ bid for Mannesmann.

2 After _merging_ with an Italian company, we had to re-assess our language training needs.

3 The chairman told shareholders that accepting the offer would lead to long-term _growth (benefits)_ in sales.

4 The merger will help us to secure a _competitive_ advantage over our biggest rivals.

5 There is no doubt that the merger will deliver substantial cost _benefits (growth)_

6 To fight a hostile bid, the company announced plans to _restructure (streamline)_ the workforce by cutting 2000 jobs.

7 The move led to a major _streamlining (restructuring)_ programme, especially in duplicated areas such as administration.

8 After a period of major expansion through _acquisition_, we began to lose focus of our core activities.

3 Match the words as they appear in the unit.

1 achieve — operating — of scale
2 integrate — economies — value
3 add — different — prices
4 undercut — cost — improvements
5 reduce — long-term — cultures
6 generate — competitors' — costs

4 Fill each gap with a suitable word.

Advanced Technologies plc, the automobile components manufacturer, yesterday agreed (**1**) _to_ consider an offer from the French-based Avignon Group of 68p a share. This latest bid, which (**2**) _contains_ an increase of 13p on their original offer, beats (**3**) _____ of German rival Hellman AG, who last week offered 60p a share. The bid values Advanced at £19m, almost twice (**4**) _the_ market capitalisation when it was floated in 1996. It is not yet clear (**5**) _if_ Hellman will return with a counterbid. Advanced Chairman Tom McGillis said the company would (**6**) _not_ contact any other parties for two weeks (**7**) _before_ it considered Avignon's newest offer. An Avignon spokesman said that the merger would deliver immediate benefits to the company (**8**) _____ as cost savings and long-term sustainable shareholder value.

Relative pronouns

5 Complete the text by filling each gap with a suitable relative pronoun. Add any necessary commas.

The merger raises a number of HR issues (**1**) _which/that_ will need to be addressed as a matter of urgency and in a manner (**2**) _which_ is seen to be fair to the employees of both companies. Firstly the pay structures of the two companies (**3**) _which_ show marked differences will need to be reviewed and harmonised. Furthermore redundancy terms will have to be agreed and offered to employees (**4**) _who_ lose their jobs as a result of the merger. This is particularly important with regard to senior managers (**5**) _whose_ contracts contain severance clauses (**6**) _which_ guarantee them generous terms. Our approach to these job cuts (**7**) _which_ were promised to shareholders as part of the terms of the merger will also have a major effect on staff morale within the newly-formed company. It is imperative that we avoid any deterioration of staff morale (**8**) _which_ could have an adverse effect on company performance.

Reading Test Part Two

- Read the letter replying to an enquiry about conference facilities.
- Choose the best sentence from **A - H** to fill in each of the gaps.
- For each gap **1 - 6**, mark **one** letter **A - H**.
- Do not use any letter more than once.
- There is an example at the beginning **(0)**.

Dear

I was delighted to meet you at the UK Conference Exhibition last week in Bath and I would like to take the opportunity to thank you for the interest you have shown in the wide range of conference centres we represent. **0** | H | Photographs of our superb centre can be viewed on our website at www.devonshiremanor.co.uk.

Devonshire Manor is set in 100 acres of private woodland and gardens approximately 10 miles south of Exeter city centre and just seven miles from the M5 motorway. **1** | D | Despite the changes, Devonshire Manor has managed to retain the atmosphere of a traditional English country estate.

Devonshire Manor provides the ideal venue for both conferences and meetings of up to 40 delegates. **2** | C | These gardens are an immensely popular setting for functions such as open-air press conferences and product launches. The meeting rooms themselves are completely self-contained, with full air-conditioning and sound-proofing. **3** | E | Flip charts, overhead projectors, whiteboards, TVs and videos are all included as standard. Facsimile and photocopying facilities are also available at an extra cost.

Devonshire Manor has 20 en suite bedrooms, all of which are beautifully furnished and contain a writing desk, colour TV, radio, direct dial telephone and minibar. We hope that delegates find time to enjoy the wealth of activities which both the Devonshire Manor estate and its surroundings have to offer. **4** | F | After a hard day's work, such leisure facilities provide guests with the perfect opportunity to unwind.

Delegate rates start at £125 pp + VAT, based on 24-hour mid-week occupancy. **5** | G | The price also includes parking and unlimited use of the leisure facilities during your stay at Devonshire Manor. **6** | A | Alternatively, if you would like to discuss your particular requirements with us in more detail, we would be pleased to meet you. In the meantime, if you have any questions regarding the above information, please do not hesitate to contact me on (01392) 548697.

I look forward to hearing from you.

Yours sincerely

A   For a quotation for your company's proposed conference, please complete the enclosed form.

B   This is the reason why we give all delegates access to video data projectors and other visual aids.

C   In addition to the house itself, there is also a beautiful terrace overlooking award-winning grounds.

D   The large 17th century house has been tastefully renovated and refurbished to provide all the amenities of a modern conference centre.

E   An extensive range of conference equipment is provided in each one.

F   In addition to a nine-hole golf course, Devonshire Manor has four tennis courts, an outdoor heated swimming pool and a sauna.

G   This covers the use of conference rooms and standard equipment as well as full-board accommodation.

H   In response to your enquiry regarding Devonshire Manor, I enclose full details concerning the facility.

Reading Test Part Four

- Read the memo below about sales people's performance.
- Choose the best word to fill each gap.
- For each question **1 - 10**, mark **one** letter **A**, **B**, **C** or **D**.
- There is an example at the beginning **(0)**.

Salesperson of the month

Our salesperson of the month is Kurt Steiner from Stuttgart, who wins four bottles of the finest champagne. Kurt achieved sales worth € 150,000, which means that he **(0)** ..A.. his monthly target by over € 40,000. Congratulations Kurt!

There was another excellent performance in Switzerland from Cécile Fourget, who almost won the prize on account of her **(1)** ..C.. high sales figures throughout June. Another Swiss salesperson with very good **(2)** ..A.. in June was Marie Dupont, with total sales of more than € 130,000.

After a bad start to the month, sales in London **(3)** ..A.. swiftly, mainly due to the superb performance of Mike McGillis. Mike was successful in winning a major **(4)** ..C.. with LTV Production, which will be worth over € 120,000 for the company.

In France, Claudette Le Blanc from Lyon sold € 70,000 worth of business. This will obviously go a long **(5)** ..D.. towards increasing the turnover of one of our newest sites, which has been forced to **(6)** ..C.. at a loss for the last six months. Our Lisieux centre has also done well, with one of the newest **(7)** ..A.. of our French sales team, Jérome Zola, selling € 50,000 worth of business.

As for Finland, our **(8)** ..D.. figures suggest that sales are well down compared to the same period last year. However, we expect that the situation will **(9)** ..B.. quickly once the recession is over.

Finally, just a reminder that our bonus scheme runs until the end of this week, so get your **(10)** ..B.. out to clients as quickly as possible. Who knows, you might be our next 'Salesperson of the month'!

Example

0　A　exceeded　　B　excelled　　C　overtook　　D　overcame

A　B　C　D

1	A usually	B regularly	C consistently	D evenly
2	A levels	B results	C grades	D marks
3	A recovered	B regained	C restored	D repaired
4	A commission	B agreement	C contract	D arrangement
5	A route	B distance	C run	D way
6	A manage	B act	C operate	D work
7	A members	B delegates	C associates	D partners
8	A immediate	B actual	C instant	D current
9	A increase	B improve	C enlarge	D elevate
10	A statements	B invoices	C charges	D accounts

Reading Test Part Five

- Read the article below about industrial action at a bank.
- For each question 1 - 10, write **one** word.

Example

0 | T | H | E | | | | | |

Bank says strike fails to make impact

Newham Bank and two major finance unions were fighting a war of words yesterday over the impact of a long-running pay dispute. A spokesman for the BBU, **(0)** *the* larger of the two unions, claimed that a second 24-hour strike **(1)** *had* had a serious impact on the bank's operations and that support for industrial action was growing. An estimated 28,000 staff walked out on Wednesday, causing **(2)** *what* the union called 'serious disruption'.

These claims, however, have been branded **(3)** *as* 'nonsense' by Newham. The bank said that fewer than 100 branches had closed **(4)** *out* of a total of over 1,500 and that the number of people taking part in the strike had been only about 4,000. The bank also denied claims by the unions that the action had put as **(5)** *many* as half its 2,000 cash machines out of service and caused delays to mortgage and loan authorisations.

'We're delighted at having had **(6)** *such* a great response from members,' said BBU official Amanda Conroy. 'There's absolutely **(7)** *no* doubt that this is having a very serious impact on Newham's operations.' The bank, on the other hand, said, 'The strike has had little or no impact on services in most areas of the country and almost **(8)** *all* our 56,000 staff are working as normal.'

The dispute began when the bank announced plans to implement a performance-based pay scheme, **(9)** *which* the unions maintain will lead to an effective pay freeze for 25,000 of **(10)** *their* members. However, the bank insists that the new scheme is a fairer way of rewarding hard-working employees.

Reading Test Part Six (A)

- In **most** lines of the following text, there is **one** unnecessary word. It is either grammatically incorrect or does not fit in with the sense of the text.
- For each numbered line 1 - 12, find the unnecessary word. Some lines are correct. If a line is correct, write **CORRECT**.
- The exercise begins with two examples **(0)** and **(00)**.

Example

0 | C | O | R | R | E | C | T | | |

00 | T | H | I | S | | | | | |

Newsletter

0	Just one year after moving into the suburbs of Stockholm, our largest
00	Swedish branch this has outgrown its current premises. The centre will be
1	moving again in the next few weeks, this time order to purpose-built
2	offices in the city centre. Business has grown by more than a fifty per cent
3	during the past year. Moreover, the branch has recently been gained a
4	prestigious new contract with one of the city's major accountancy firms,
5	currently outsourcing its management training. The contract which will
6	initially be for a two-year period but we hope it will be extended. What
7	helped us win the contract was in the success of the training we have
8	been doing for similar companies in the recent years. Even though it is not
9	yet clear how big the contract will be, but it is expected to grow steadily
10	as more and more management training is gradually outsourced. We are
11	positive the excellent new location will be provide further boosts, both to
12	sales and morale. We would like to take this chance to thank you staff and
	management for their efforts over the last twelve months.

Reading Test Part Six (B)

- In **most** lines of the following text, there is **one** unnecessary word. It is either grammatically incorrect or does not fit in with the sense of the text.
- For each numbered line **1 - 12**, find the unnecessary word. Some lines are correct. If a line is correct, write **CORRECT**.
- The exercise begins with two examples **(0)** and **(00)**.

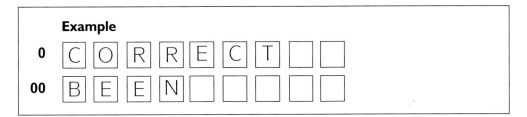

Example

0 | C | O | R | R | E | C | T | | |

00 | B | E | E | N | | | | | |

0	One of the most effective ways to learn a language is to take a course in
00	the country where it is been spoken. That is why more and more
1	business and professional people they are attending language training
2	courses overseas rather than in their own country. Although such courses
3	may be expensive, participants have the opportunity to work on
4	developing their skills every minute of the day. In addition to have formal
5	lessons, participants have the opportunity to learn in social situations with
6	trainers and fellow students. Staying with a host family that gives
7	participants even more of exposure to the target language and helps them
8	make immediate use of the language they have learned. A course
9	overseas not only gives to participants the perfect way of experiencing the
10	cultural life of the country at a first hand. It also provides an opportunity for them
11	to make network with their counterparts and gain valuable insights which
12	will help them for operate more effectively in the global arena which is
	international business today.

Trade fairs

Exhibiting at a trade fair

Speaking ❶ What are the benefits of trade fairs for exhibitors and visitors?

[handwritten notes:]
- making contacts with possible buyers and retailers
- high frequency of people passing by
- only interested visitors

exhibitors

[handwritten notes:]
- comparison of different offers
- no waste of time in travelling around
- knowing what is state of the art (top-notch)?

Earls Court Two Exhibition Centre, London

Reading 1 ❷ Read the advertisement. What details are given about the following?

the exhibition	the exhibitors	the visitors
what? - design home accessories *- personal gift items* *when? 3 days in May summer + autumn* *550 exhibitors*	*- high standard* *- quality products* *- innovative* *- hand-picked for talent + originality* *- 150 newbies* *55*	*- 20'000 visitors* *- international + UK* *- ahead of competition*

Top Drawer Summer
7th - 9th May 2000
Earls Court Two, London

top drawer
LONDON

Top Drawer Summer is THE event of the season for design-led home accessories and personal gift items. We continually watch the market for companies like yours who share the high standards of the Top Drawer exhibition and the quality of the products displayed at the show.

For three days in May, Earls Court Two is the centre of creativity, with 550 of Europe's most innovative exhibitors showing the ideas that are making their reputations. Every company has been hand-picked for talent and originality. More than 150 exhibitors will be attending Top Drawer Summer for the first time, giving buyers a unique chance to meet the people who will be making tomorrow's headlines.

Both summer and autumn exhibitions attract 20,000 UK and international quality buyers who visit Top Drawer because they know it provides them with new, interesting products and supplies. It is the key show for buyers, keeping them ahead of the competition.

Can you afford not to be seen there?

[handwritten notes:]
supply and demand
Angebot + Nachfrage

Speaking **3** Your company wishes to exhibit at a trade fair. Discuss and decide the following.

- your objectives for the trade fair
- where and when you should exhibit

Live '98 exhibition at Earls Court, London

Replying to an enquiry

Speaking **1** What information might trade fair organisers include in a standard letter of reply to enquiries about an exhibition? - *prices per square metre (m²)*
- amenities: (electricity, water, heating)
- accessability

Reading 2 **2** Your teacher will give you Top Drawer's standard reply to enquiries. Put the sentences into the correct order. Then divide the letter into paragraphs.

top drawer
LONDON

3 Now read the Top Drawer letter and compare your answer.

Top Drawer Summer 7th - 9th May 2000
Earls Court Two, London

Dear

Thank you for your interest in the above event. As requested, I enclose full details of this and future shows for you.

Held in Central London, Top Drawer attracts buyers who understand the importance of good design and new products. If you rely on meeting customers face to face in an environment that allows you to show your products to their best advantage, you will not be disappointed.

Now in its eighteenth year, Top Drawer continues to be the showcase event for personal gifts and home accessories. Both summer and autumn exhibitions attract some 20,000 UK and overseas buyers from independent retailers, department stores, mail order houses and contract interior designers.

The key to the continuing popularity of Top Drawer is its selection process, ensuring that buyers are seeing the very best in the industry. Consequently, we ask for all new applications to be accompanied by a brochure, photographs or samples.

Top Drawer is such a popular show that by the time this letter reaches you, many of the available stands will already have been rebooked. Therefore, we recommend you reserve your stand as soon as possible and we guarantee all applications will be given our full attention the moment we receive them.

If you require any further information or advice, please do not hesitate to call Adrian Gwyn-Evans, Lisa Ferguson or myself on **020 7370 8350**.

I look forward to hearing from you.

Yours sincerely

Isobelle Dennis
Sales Manager

EARLS COURT EXHIBITION CENTRE WARWICK ROAD LONDON SW5 9TA TEL: +44 (0) 20 7370 8210 OR FAX: +44 (0) 20 7370 8235
INTERNET: http://www.eco.co.uk/poevent/topdraw EMAIL: topdrawer@eco.co.uk

4 Look at the letter again and find examples of the following.

standard letter phrases   main points

organisation of letters

supporting ideas   linking words

Language **5** Look at the following sentence. Find further examples in the letter of the present simple referring to future time.

*All applications will be given our full attention the moment we **receive** them.*

6 Complete the following information with phrases from the Top Drawer letter.

Standard letter phrases

The following phrases are useful when writing letters.

- **Referring to an earlier letter or conversation**
  With reference to your letter dated ... in which ...
  Further to our conversation of ...

  _____

- **Enclosing**
  Please find enclosed ...

  _____

- **Offering assistance**
  Should you have any further questions, please contact me on ...

  _____

- **Referring to future contact**
  We look forward to meeting you on ...

  _____

Writing **7** Write a 200-250 word letter of reply to an enquiry received by your company. Give details about the company's products/services and prices. Consider the following.

- who the reader is and what information is needed
- the purpose, order and content of paragraphs
- your main points and supporting ideas in each paragraph

Boat show '98 at Earls Court, London

Optional task **8** Research a trade fair of interest to your company. Write a 200-250 word report describing the event and recommending why your company should exhibit there.

Entering a market

Researching a market

Speaking ❶ What research would a company do before entering a foreign market?

(handwritten notes)
- language
- selling potential, demand, costumers
- qualified staff
- production prices / costs
- laws, regulation, taxes / legal situation
- competitors
- distribution channels, retailers / retail outlets
- land prices to build manufacturing plant
- buying power
- GNP gross national product
  Brutto inlandprodukt
- import tariff duties
- currency
- culture / tradition / religion / etiquette / ethics
- publicity / promotion / PR
- political situation
- average income
- clients
- interest rates (Zins)

Reading ❷ Read the text on the opposite page. Where do you think it is from? Who is the text aimed at?

❸ Read the text again and answer the following questions.

1 Why is the UK so important to China?
2 Which industries in China offer most potential for UK companies?
3 What ways are there to enter the Chinese market?
4 Which qualities are necessary for success in China?
5 Why is it advisable for exporters to visit China?

Doing business in China

China, with one fifth of the world's population and one of the fastest rates of economic growth, is a major target for global business. Direct UK exports to China amounted to £928.2 million in 1997; exports to China via Hong Kong were worth another £697 million. With pledged investment of US $12 billion, the UK is acknowledged to be the leading European investor in China and the main EU source of technology. We can now build on this base to increase our exports and to develop our commercial interests.

Our strengths match China's needs, particularly in telecommunications, financial services, aviation and environmental technology. Substantial opportunities also exist in a wide range of other sectors and the chances are that companies with profiles similar to your own are already doing business with the Chinese, either directly or through Hong Kong.

There are a number of different strategies for entering the Chinese market. Agents or distributors in Hong Kong are often able to generate sales in mainland China, particularly in the south, but there is a growing private sector within China itself. Agents and distributors are still a rarity, however, and most business is done by identifying end users and/or possible joint venture partners. Success in China will require long term commitment and the ability to research the market thoroughly and forge relationships with the Chinese themselves. Companies with previous experience of exporting (particularly to other parts of Asia) who are willing to participate in trade fairs in China and who are prepared to produce trade literature in Chinese will have the greatest chance of success. It will almost always be necessary to visit the market as the Chinese very rarely respond to mailshots or requests for information by fax from unknown sources. Further visits to China will be necessary as business partnerships develop.

中英携手共创未来

Britain 合 China

Language **4** Look at the articles (*a, an, the*) in the text. What main differences do you note between the use of articles in English and your language?

Speaking **5** Choose one of the topics below and talk about it for one minute. Before you begin, think about the following.

main points	supporting ideas	introduction	conclusion

- how to research a new export market
- the importance of good preparation for a business trip

Business practices in China

Listening ❶ Tanya Liddell, a successful exporter, addresses a local business association about doing business in China. Listen and complete the notes using up to three words or a number.

On arrival in China

1 There are few universally accepted business norms in China as _standards and expectations_ vary throughout the country.

2 It is essential to do thorough _(extension) preparatory work_ ✓ preparatory before visiting China.

3 It is viewed as extremely rude if you are _late for meetings_ in China. ✓ discourteous discourteous

4 When travelling from your hotel, always take into account the severe _congestion ? (bottleneck)_ _(traffic) congestion_ in Chinese cities.

5 Upon arrival, you will normally be met by a _host / manager_ and fellow staff. ✓ usually senior

Meetings

6 First of all, everyone exchanges _business cards_ with one another. ✓

7 The host will then formally open the meeting with a _brief introduction_ to the ✓ company and its operations.

8 Visitors should notify their hosts in advance if they intend to use _audio-visual aids_. ✓

Socialising

9 Chinese hosts usually organise a _dinner_ for foreign visitors. ✓ special

10 A good topic of conversation is to enquire about your host's _(family) children_ ✓

11 The Chinese feel an obligation to provide _(harmony and family)_ at all times. hospitality ?

12 They will often arrange _sightseeing_ for visitors.

Speaking ❷ What advice would you give Chinese people visiting your country on business?

You have received the following letter from a business acquaintance in China. Read the letter and write a 200-250 word reply.

on china

Floor 1A
Beijing Commercial Centre
9 Chang Road, Beijing
China

15 March 2000

Dear

I do not know if you remember me but we met at the RC Mandarin Hotel in Shanghai last month. You gave me your business card and kindly offered to help me if I ever planned to visit your country.

I am pleased to say I will be attending a trade fair in your city next month. I am in the process of making my travel arrangements and, as it is my first trip to your country, I would appreciate it if you could give me some advice.

In particular, I would welcome your advice on accommodation and how to get around the city. Should I arrange car hire, for example? Also, as I will have my evenings free, could you recommend places to eat? I will have a free day for sightseeing as well. What would you suggest I do?

I hope we can meet during my visit. I would very much like to invite you for a meal one evening if it is convenient.

Thank you again for your help. I hope to hear from you soon.

Regards

Chen Zhang

Optional task **4** Visit the www.biztravel.com website. Choose a destination and prepare a brief presentation on where to stay, what to do and where to eat there.

1 Some of the following lines contain an unnecessary word. Underline any extra words in lines 1-12.

1 With a reference to your letter dated 13 November, in
2 which you requested information about our forthcoming
3 exhibition 'Management in Action', please do find
4 enclosed details about this and future events in the region.
5 'Management in Action' which is the showcase event for
6 the region's major business training organisations. This
7 year's exhibition it includes thirty free taster workshops,
8 covering these areas such as motivation, health and safety,
9 team-building, presentation skills and e-commerce. If you
10 require any further information, and please do not
11 hesitate to contact either myself or Elizabeth Wellington
12 on 01952 345642. We are look forward to hearing from
you in the near future.

2 Complete the puzzle. Which words run vertically through the answers?

1. A D V E R T I S E M E N T
2. R E P L Y
3. A P P L I C A T I O N
4. D E S I G N
5. E
6. B E N E F I T S
7. S T A N D S
8. I
9. B R O C H U R E S

1 Organisers can promote an exhibition by placing an
_ad_ in a newspaper or magazine.

2 Exhibition organisers often respond to enquiries with
a standard letter of _reply_ .

3 Companies interested in exhibiting have to complete
an _application_ form and send samples.

4 The _design_ of the stand and publicity material
needs to fit in with our corporate image.

5 Earls Court hosts many top international _____
throughout the year.

6 One of the main _benefits_ for exhibitors is the
chance to meet customers face to face.

7 Exhibition organisers often reserve a number of
stands for first time exhibitors.

8 Buyers come from independent _____ as well as
large department stores.

9 At an exhibition, visitors can see the actual goods
rather than just photos in _brochures_ .

3 Re-arrange the words to make formal phrases from written correspondence.

1 enclosed / please / find
Please find enclosed

2 letter / of / to / reference / with / your
with reference to your letter of ?

3 look / meeting / we / forward / to / you
we look forward to meeting you

4 to / our / conversation / further / of
to our further conversation of

5 further / questions / should / have / you / any
should you have any further questions

6 not / do / please / me / hesitate / contact / to
please do not hesitate to contact me

Time clauses

4 Complete the conversation. Put each verb in brackets into the correct form.

● Hi Ross, it's Jan. I hear (**1** you/go) _you're going_
to the trade fair in Poznan next week.

▼ Yes. How about you?

● No, I'm not. But Monica's asked me to give you
some details about travel arrangements and so on.

▼ Oh right, great.

● Do you have a pen ready?

▼ Sure, fire away.

● Right. Your plane (**2** land) _will land_ at
Poznan at 10.20 on Thursday. It's flight BA442. When
you (**3** get) _get_ there, you'll be met
at the airport by Sergiusz Jablonski.

▼ Will I be going into meetings as soon as I (**4** arrive)
arrive or am I going to the hotel first?

● Sergiusz (**5** take) _will take_ you to your
hotel. Once you (**6** check in) _have checked in_ ,
he'll take you to lunch with some of the managers.

▼ OK. Is there anything planned for the evening?

● I'd imagine so, but they haven't sent us any details.
I'm sure Sergiusz will let you know what's going on
when you (**7** get) _get_ there.

▼ OK. Let's see now. Is there anything else I need to
know before I (**8** go) _go_ ?

● I think that's about it. Your return flight's at 11.55 the
next morning, so you'll have plenty of time to have a
relaxed breakfast and make your way to the airport in
good time.

1 Find words in the unit which go after *business*.

business   partnership
              partner
              relation
              administration
              lunch

2 Complete the sentences with the following words.

amount to	respond to	enquire about
allow for	participate in	intend to
	invest in	build on

1 Many UK financial service companies are particularly keen to _*invest in*_ China.

2 Ensure that you warn your hosts in advance if you _*intend to*_ use audio-visual equipment.

3 This year direct UK exports to China are estimated to _*amount to*_ well over £1bn.

4 Having entered China, many UK companies are now looking to _*build on*_ their success.

5 When entering the Chinese market, a company has to _*enquire about*_ regional differences. *allow for?*

6 Another tip for companies is to _*participate in*_ as many local trade fairs and exhibitions as possible.

7 Mailshots are not advisable as the Chinese rarely _*respond to*_ them.

8 Visitors should _*allow~~ enquire about*_ the host's children as the family counts above all else in China.

3 Put the following words into the correct group.

an arrangement	a mailshot	business
conversation	a joint venture	an investment
a partnership	a request	research
a commitment	a relationship	preparatory work

make	do	enter into
an arrangement	*a mailshot*	*conversation*
business	*an investment*	*a joint venture*
a request	*research*	*a partnership*
a commitment	*preparatory work*	*a relationship*

4 Look at the information comparing average prices in London and Beijing. Write a 120-140 word report comparing the cost of doing business in the two cities.

Index (London = 100)	0	50	100	150	200

Average cost of one night in a 5-star hotel

Average cost of office space per sq. metre

Average wage of a bilingual secretary

Average monthly rent for a small apartment

The cost of a 5-minute local phone call

5 Match the words as they appear in the unit.

1 generate   business cards
2 forge   sales
3 pledge   needs
4 produce   proceedings
5 swap   hospitality
6 provide   investment
7 start   trade literature
8 match   relationships

Articles

6 Complete the text by adding the necessary articles.

At meetings with *the* Chinese, *the* leader of your group will be expected to enter first and will generally be offered *a* seat beside *the* most senior Chinese person present. This person will usually chair *the* meeting and act as *the* host. At *the* beginning of *the* meeting, all *the* people present will greet each other and swap business cards, after which *a* period of small talk begins. *The* Host will then officially start *the* proceedings with *a* brief introduction to *the* Chinese enterprise. *The* Visiting team is then invited to speak. It is appropriate at this point for foreign participants to make their case and answer questions. Following *the* meeting *the* Chinese enterprise will probably arrange *a* special dinner for *the* overseas guests along with other entertainment such as sightseeing. Guests should always accept these invitations as small talk in *a* social setting is essential for forging relationships with *the* Chinese.

Reading Test Part Three

- Read the following article on investing in shares and the questions on the opposite page.
- Each question has four suggested answers or ways of finishing the sentence, **A**, **B**, **C** and **D**.
- Mark **one** letter **A**, **B**, **C** or **D** for the answer you choose.

Investing in the stock market has always been more profitable than putting money into a traditional savings account. However, it is only in the last few years that private share ownership has become accepted as a reliable form of investment. There are many reasons why more and more people are now buying shares. To begin with, the whole process is now far more flexible and user-friendly and public awareness of investment products and their tax implications is a lot higher. Even more importantly, this awareness means people now realise that in the medium to long term shares are far more lucrative than deposit accounts. Today, people are also more likely to invest in a company for ethical reasons or as a show of support for that company.

When deciding to invest in shares, it is essential to think about your objectives. In order to avoid an expensive mistake, you need to consider your existing short and long-term financial commitments and how quickly you expect to see a return on your investment. Most importantly, you need to decide the extent to which you are prepared to speculate and then select the investment products which best reflect your attitude towards the perils inherent in any stock market investment.

Recently, newspapers have been full of stories of investors realising massive profits, usually in connection with the flood of Internet companies that have issued shares in the last twelve months. Such companies, however, are anything but a safe investment. Although people have been attracted by the phenomenal rate at which these companies are expanding, many investors have seen their shares fall well below the issue price within months of buying them.

Private investors unwilling to tolerate high levels of risk can reduce this uncertainty by buying shares in blue chip companies, which are established organisations such as banks or large international corporations. Although such an investment may minimise risk, it also limits the potential profits. Some investors try to remove the element of risk by closely monitoring stock market movements on a daily basis or by paying a regular sum into a managed fund over a long period of time. However, no matter how carefully people follow the markets or what expert advice they receive, statistics show that the safest option is to spread risk by investing in a wide range of different companies across different sectors.

As a first-time investor, it is vital to seek professional advice. Consultants can provide information on how to invest in the most attractive companies in both the UK and overseas. They can explain how stocks, shares, unit trusts and bonds actually work, how much each type of investment costs and, most importantly, which products best match their clients' requirements.

One reliable way of managing investments is through a broker, who charges a brokerage fee in the form of a percentage of the money invested. An alternative method is to deal in shares on the Internet. This incurs none of the regular broker's commission and investors can therefore easily afford to buy and sell shares more regularly. However, although some potential investors may find on-line trading exciting, they should be aware that direct trading is perhaps the least secure way of approaching the stock market, with few investors having the necessary skills and knowledge to make any profit whatsoever, never mind the fortunes popularised by the media.

1 According to the text, more people are now buying shares because

    A more ethical investments are available.

    B investors get a better rate of return. ✓

    C investment periods are more flexible. (✓)

    D investors pay less tax on earnings.

2 What is the main consideration when deciding to invest in shares?

    A how much you pay for the shares

    B how quickly you can make a profit

    C how willing you are to take risks ✓

    D how financially secure you are

3 Investors are attracted to Internet companies because they

    A sell their shares at a low price.

    B have a large number of shares.

    C are often a very safe investment.

    D offer potential for rapid growth. ✓

4 Investors can reduce risk and still make good profits by

    A investing only in blue chip companies.

    B monitoring share prices very closely.

    C buying shares gradually over time.

    D choosing a variety of investments. ✓

5 What is the most useful advice for new investors?

    A the best time to invest in shares

    B the most suitable type of investment ✓

    C the cheapest way to buy shares

    D the safest companies to invest in

6 Many investors buy and sell shares via the Internet because it is

    A far cheaper. ✓

    B much easier.

    C more exciting. (✓)

    D a lot safer.

Writing Test Part Two

- A friend of yours has applied for a new job which is similar to your current position. You have just received a letter asking you for a written reference.
- Write a **letter** of reference for your friend. Refer to relevant factors such as current responsibilities, personal qualities and suitability for the new position.
- Write **200 - 250** words.

The future of work

Visions

Reading 1 ❶ Read the extract from a magazine article about the future of work and answer the questions.

his is as good as it gets. The golden beach, the crystal clear water and the gentle refreshing breeze. You knew working from Sri Lanka for a few months would be a good idea, but this is paradise. Suddenly your pleasant thoughts are interrupted by your pager - the meeting, of course! Lying on the beach, you'd forgotten all about it. Quickly, you gather your things and head back to the rented beach house. You walk through the terrace doors and shout at your personal work organiser to download any mail and access all the meeting preparation files. On the wall a large flat monitor hums and flickers into life as you head into the shower. You walk back into the room to see your team leader's face on the wall giving details about the marketing project and today's objectives. You try to pinpoint exactly what it is about him that you dislike, but you can't. Not that it matters, of course, because in six weeks the project will be over and you'll probably never see his face on your wall again. Your work organiser has already scanned the Web and applied for several new assignments. It knows what work you want to do and how much you expect to earn. It then does the rest for you - searching through the thousands of vacancies on the Web and selecting those most compatible with your CV, which, of course, it updates automatically before submitting. You forget the briefing for a moment and gaze out across the terrace at the waves gently lapping against the shore. Did people really use to work in the same office all their lives?

1   What year do you think the author is writing about?
2   What would be the advantages/disadvantages of this lifestyle?
3   Do you think this way of working will become reality?
4   Would you like to have this lifestyle?

Predictions

Reading 2 ❶ Five managers make predictions about the future of work. Look at the statements they make. Match each of the statements with one of the managers below.

1 People will work for more than one company at a time. C
2 People will want to have more free time in the future. E
3 There will be a lot more concern about health in the workplace. B
4 As work becomes more flexible, people will work longer hours. A
5 Governments will find it difficult to collect revenue from workers and companies. D
6 Companies will have to ensure that communications remain polite. C
7 Companies will be more closely involved with local communities. B
8 Large organisations will become more powerful than some governments. E

A Jeanne Desaill - Director, MAS

In future, work space will become less rigid, with hotdesking being the norm. People will expect a better standard of working environment too. There's likely to be more shift work, partly to make better use of office equipment but also to offer services around the clock. In fact, I think working hours will probably change quite dramatically. For instance, there'll be no guarantee of free time even at the weekend. Some of the business community worry that staff won't work unless supervised but the real issue will be recognising when staff are overtaxing themselves.

B Joshua Golder - Institute of Employment Studies

People are beginning to make the connection between lifestyle, performance and sickness, so I think we're bound to see a move towards promoting lifestyle issues in the office. We're already seeing this in the US, where smokers are coming under increasing pressure to change their behaviour. There'll also undoubtedly be a lot of larger companies realising the importance of their social obligations. Smart firms are already pushing these responsibilities up the agenda and showing a lot more interest in the needs of people in their immediate environment.

C Megan O'Riordan - Client Director, Dewbury Newton Carter

In future, part-time staff may be working for one employer in the morning and a different one in the afternoon, so values and branding will definitely need to be stronger. Staff interaction will be through telecommunications rather than the place of work. However, technology such as e-mail has an impact on things like style and formality and old courtesies tend to disappear. So one requirement for a healthy organisation is certainly going to be maintaining respect in relationships.

D Janice Watson - Staffordshire Teleworking Community

Companies will have to concentrate more on establishing employee loyalty, which will be hard won, with many people preferring to improve their CVs and move on to another company rather than get stressed out in their current job. Another issue is that with the growth in teleworking, how are authorities going to cope when all their taxation systems depend entirely on location? There's also no longer any clear distinction between employed and self-employed and, the way things are going, this distinction is set to disappear altogether.

E Scott Forrest - Director, Cyber Office

With people working from anywhere, there'll be a great change in employee demands in terms of contractual arrangements and the lifestyles of working people. They'll demand a healthier balance between work and leisure as it becomes less obvious when work 'stops'. What I'm worried about, however, is the erosion of people's rights if they're working for a huge company where there's little personal communication. And on a more global scale, how will a single state control a multinational which has far more resources and a lot more money?

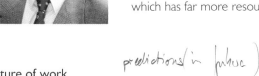

Language ❷ Look at the five texts again. How many different ways of expressing predictions can you find? Put the predictions in order of strength.

Speaking ❸ Look at the eight statements on the previous page. Which of them do you agree with?

Reality

Listening ❶ Change Management Consultant Jan Dunn talks about British Airways' new Waterside premises. Listen and choose one letter for the correct answer.

Jan Dunn
British Airways plc

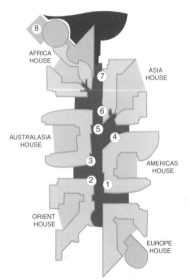

Key
1 Information point
2 Bank
3 Waitrose
4 Pavement café
5 The square
6 Cyber café
7 Espresso bar
8 Barbecue area

1 British Airways moved to the Waterside site because it
— A wanted to centralise its operations.
  B had to vacate the Heathrow site.
  C was able to save money by doing so.

2 What was the main objective of the BA vision?
  A to have a more co-operative environment
  B to allow people to work more flexibly
  C to centralise its information and data

3 What example of reduced hierarchy does Jan Dunn give?
  A executives being allocated smaller offices
  B senior managers losing their parking spaces
  C managers sharing their personal assistants

4 Why does BA want residents to use the Street every day?
  A to increase the security of the building
  B to encourage a sense of community
  C to promote trade at the Street shop

5 How can residents be contacted within the building?
  A They receive messages from their department.
  B They can be called to information points.
  C They key personal numbers into any phone.

British Airways, Waterside

6   BA provides high street facilities at Waterside because
    A   they are a source of income.
    B   it saves time during the day.
    C   there are no facilities nearby.

7   The company is changing its meetings culture by
    A   holding all large meetings in the main theatre.
    B   encouraging people to hold smaller meetings.
    C   promoting the use of cafés for meetings.

8   What changes has working at Waterside made to Jan Dunn's day?
    A   She works a lot more efficiently.
    B   She uses computers more often.
    C   She spends less time in meetings.

Speaking ❷   **Look at the results of a survey about how residents adapted to working at Waterside in the first twelve months. How did the move change working conditions for BA staff?**

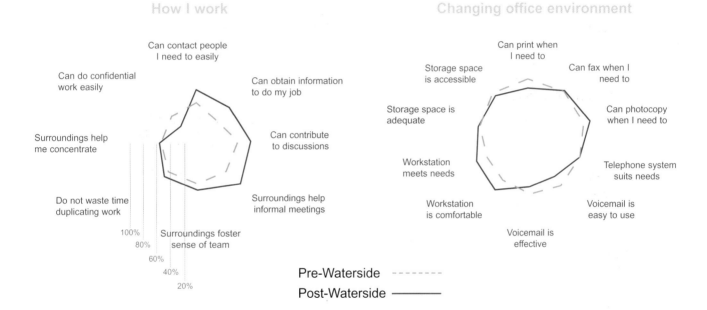

How I work

Can contact people
I need to easily

Can do confidential
work easily

Can obtain information
to do my job

Surroundings help
me concentrate

Can contribute
to discussions

Do not waste time
duplicating work

Surroundings help
informal meetings

100%
80%
60%
40%
20%

Surroundings foster
sense of team

Changing office environment

Can print when
I need to

Storage space
is accessible

Can fax when I
need to

Storage space is
adequate

Can photocopy
when I need to

Workstation
meets needs

Telephone system
suits needs

Workstation
is comfortable

Voicemail is
easy to use

Voicemail is
effective

Pre-Waterside   - - - - - - -
Post-Waterside ————

❸   **Work in pairs. Find out about the way your partner works using the *How I work* diagram above. What would your partner like to change most?**

Optional task ❹   **Visit the www.british-airways.com website and write a 200-250 word summary of the company's mission, values and goals.**

e-business

What is e-business?

Speaking ❶ How often do you use the Internet and for what reasons?

daily

e-banking, buying+importing CD's, information

Reading ❷ Read the information on the opposite page from IBM's website. What is the difference between e-business and e-commerce? What are the benefits of each?

take tightening relationship   *cheaper, faster*

g more benefit

❸ Which of these words is used most frequently in the text?

technology	business	commerce	customer	Internet
	9	3	16	

Speaking ❹ What difficulties might be experienced with e-business and e-commerce?

national law, payments solutions&security,

What is e-business?

e-busi-ness (e'biz'nis) The transformation of key business processes through the use of Internet technologies.

The Web is changing every aspect of our lives, but no area is undergoing as rapid and significant a change as the way businesses operate. Today companies large and small are using the Web to communicate with their partners, transform their order processing systems and transact commerce. This is e-business - where the strength and reliability of traditional information technology meet the Internet.

It's about business, not technology

e-business isn't about re-inventing your business. It's about streamlining your current business processes to improve operating efficiencies, which in turn will strengthen the value you provide to your customers - value that cannot be generated by any other means, and value that will give you a serious advantage over the competition.

We believe that the best place to start is with your most critical business process - customer relationship management. Start by improving your customer interactions and internal processes. To achieve this, look at the individual processes that contribute to the overall customer experience: processes such as customer relationship management, supply chain management and e-commerce.

Customers - the key ingredient to success

The concept of customer self-service is central to e-business. Analyzing past customer behaviour enables an e-business to personalize its offerings and to anticipate customer wants and needs. Providing quality customer self-service involves providing customers with secure web-browser access to automated order systems. These systems give customers controlled access to the data they need. In other words, not only are you managing your relationship with your customers, but also giving them the tools to manage their relationship with you.

Supply chain management

Supply chain management is about optimizing business processes in every corner of the business enterprise - from your supplier's supplier to your customer's customer. By using e-business concepts and Web technologies, you can manage beyond the organization. Manufacturers and vendors can share sales forecasts, manage inventories more effectively, schedule labour accordingly, optimize deliveries and improve productivity.

e-commerce

No aspect of e-business has attracted more attention than e-commerce. The ability to offer goods and services over the Web has already had a remarkable impact. Last year, for instance, over $750 million in airline tickets were sold over the Web. By using e-commerce solutions, companies can present their goods more effectively, take orders and invoice online, automate customer account enquiries and handle transactions electronically. Not only does this mean improved margins for you, but it also means your customers receive the faster, more responsive service they demand.

Taken from the www.ibm.com website

The advantages of e-business

Listening ❶ Five IBM clients talk about how Web technology has transformed an area of their business. Listen and decide which area and which benefit each speaker refers to.

Task one: area of business
Which area of business does each speaker say has been most transformed?

1 H..

2 G..

3 C..

4 D..

5 F..

A	advertising methods	Werbung
B	after-sales service	Kaufsberatung
~~C~~	client information service	Info
~~D~~	customer purchasing process	Kauf
E	production processes	Produktion
F	supply management	Lieferung
~~G~~	sales network	Vreskaufnetz
H	training methods	Tranlysnetworl

Task two: benefit
Which is the main benefit each speaker mentions?

6 J..

7 I..

8 O..

9 N..

10 (P)/N

~~I~~	improved product support
~~J~~	reduced operating costs
K	increased turnover
L	reduced staff turnover
~~M~~	increased export activity
~~N~~	reduced number of mistakes
~~O~~	improved image
P	reduced production times

SMB   small and medium businesses   = KMU

Language **2** Look at the future perfect and future continuous forms in the following sentences. Could other verb forms be used? Find further examples of these forms in the tapescript and discuss how they are used.

By the time the project's implemented, we'll have networked 300,000 employees. [future perfect]
And this year we'll be delivering up to 30 per cent of our courses by distance learning. [future continuous]

Writing **3** Look at the graph showing the predicted growth of worldwide Internet commerce. Write a 120-140 word report comparing e-business and e-commerce.

There's no business like Internet business
Emerging business model: fundamental characteristics

Industrial Age

Digital Age

Companies	Inwardly focused	Extended enterprises
Customers	Limited access to manufacturer	Direct access to manufacturer
Suppliers	'Arm's length' relationships	Electronic relationships
Intermediaries	Stand-alone entities/separate processes	Extended enterprise links/shared processes
Employees	Hierarchical and functionally managed	Empowered teams and cross-functionally managed

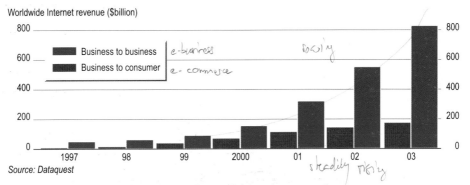
Worldwide Internet revenue ($billion)

Business to business [e-business]
Business to consumer [e-commerce]

Source: Dataquest

Taken from the Financial Times, 19 July 1999

Optional task **4** Write a 200-250 word report on a company's website. Include information about the site's strengths and weaknesses and make recommendations for its further development.

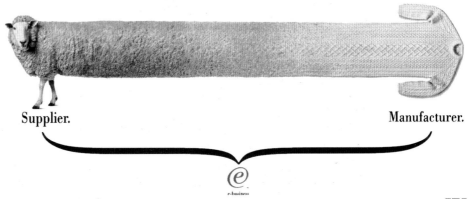
Supplier.   Manufacturer.

e-business

Production goes more smoothly when you link the steps with Internet technology. To find out more, visit www.ibm.com/e-business or call 0800 875 875

IBM
Solutions for a small planet

1 Do the following statements refer to positive or negative situations at work?

1 He's been overtaxing himself a bit lately.

2 Our new line manager's really created a team spirit. +

3 Some members of staff are struggling to cope with some of the new technology. —

4 We have noticed that old courtesies have tended to disappear since we've been using e-mail. —

5 My new workstation makes it a bit more convenient for doing any confidential work. +

6 Flexible working means there's less of a conflict between my work and home life. +

2 Choose the correct word to fill each gap.

Well, I've been here for a few months now and I'm really enjoying it. It's quite different from my last job. For one thing, the working (1) _environment_ here is definitely very different from the old company. The managers have (2) _pushed_ flexible working up the agenda and (3) _identified_ areas where it would make more (4) _sense_ to work from home. After all, if we are all (5) _logged_ onto the same network, then the (6) _location_ of your workstation doesn't really matter, does it? It's just as easy to (7) _contribute_ to a team using e-mail and the telephone. Working from home is a win-win situation because it increases efficiency and cuts the time it (8) _takes_ travelling to the office.

1 A style   B surrounding   C environment
2 A pushed   B encouraged   C promoted
3 A controlled B identified   C clarified
4 A sense   B logic   C value
5 A joined   B logged   C booked
6 A location   B workplace   C premises
7 A connect   B contribute   C co-operate
8 A lasts   B demands   C takes

3 Match the words.

1 book   premises
2 foster   a meeting room
3 key a number into   operations
4 run out of   a telephone terminal
5 show   team spirit
6 centralise   supplies
7 adapt to   interest
8 vacate   a new way of working

4 Complete each sentence with a suitable preposition.

1 There's a connection _between_ lifestyle and performance in the workplace.

2 The use of e-mail has a definite impact _on_ things like formality in the office environment.

3 We're very dependent _on_ the intranet, so if it goes down our operations are badly affected.

4 Some jobs, such as marketing, are more suited _to_ flexible working than others.

5 I bumped _into_ Sarah at the café this morning.

6 The company I'm working for now has even got a gym and a café _on_ site.

5 Match the verbs with the appropriate nouns.

	a meeting	needs	time
save	✗	✗	✓
meet	—	✓	—
spend	—	—	✓
run	✓	—	—
predict	—	✓	—
suit	—	✓	—
hold	✓	—	—
waste	—	—	✓

Predictions

6 Use the exact form of the word in brackets to rewrite the following predictions.

1 Traffic congestion could be eased by teleworking.
   (may) Teleworking may ease traffic congestion.

2 I can't imagine the office will cease to be important.
   (unlikely) It is unlikely that the office will cease to be important.

3 It looks as if the Internet's ready to explode.
   (set) It looks as if the Internet's set to explode. The Internet looks set to explode.

4 More people will want to work from home.
   (bound) More people will be bound to work from home.

5 I don't think everyone will want Internet access.
   (improbable) I think it is improbable that everyone will want Internet access.

6 Working from home is sure to increase in future.
   (undoubtedly) Undoubtedly working from home will increase in future.

4 More people are bound to want to work from home

1 Fill each gap with a suitable word.

Many companies have recently been taking their first tentative steps in the world of electronic business. Initially, they expected the Internet to be (1) _little_ more than an 'add on' to (2) _their_ current business procedures. However, companies are now discovering (3) _that_ electronic business will not just prove to be an efficient or cheaper sales channel (4) _but_ will fundamentally change the way they do business. Companies in sectors (5) _such_ as retailing or financial services are already realising substantial savings by using the Internet to encourage (6) _the_ growth of 'self-service' activities for customers and suppliers. Corporate intranets now allow staff to access training at (7) _any_ time and make travel arrangements and file expenses on-line, reducing the costs (8) _which_ are common to such processes.

2 Complete the puzzle. Which word runs vertically through the answers?

1	I	N	T	E	R	N	E	T		
2	W	E	B	S	I	T	E			
3		B	U	L	L	E	T	I	N	S
4	T	R	A	N	S	A	C	T	I	O	N	S
5	O	N	L	I	N	E				
6		I	N	T	R	A	N	E	T	
7	I	N	T	E	G	R	A	T	E	
8	B	R	O	W	S	E	R			
9	C	U	S	T	O	M	E	R	S	

1 e-business is using _Internet_ technology to transform basic business processes.

2 Most large companies now have a _website_ where customers can access product information.

3 The Internet is very flexible and allows companies to update their news _____ very quickly.

4 Many people worry about using credit cards to make financial _transactions_ over the Internet.

5 More and more people are getting connected to the Internet and then buying goods _online_ .

6 Many large companies have a secure company-wide computer network called an _Intranet_ .

7 The challenge is to _integrate_ Internet technologies into the company's business processes.

8 In order to access the World Wide Web, you need to use a web _browser_ .

9 Companies have to remember that e-business is about _customers_ and not technology.

3 Match the words as they appear in the unit.

1 take — offerings
2 manage — orders
3 improve — customer wants
4 handle — customer behaviour
5 communicate with — operating efficiencies
6 analyse — inventories
7 personalise — partners
8 anticipate — transactions

4 Match the words.

1 competitive — support
2 after-sales — advantage
3 product — turnover
4 staff — base
5 customer — learning
6 distance — service

Future perfect and future continuous

5 Use the prompts to write sentences using the future perfect and future continuous.

1 network / half our suppliers / by / end of this year
   We'll have networked half our suppliers by the end of this year.

2 do / more on-line training / in future
   We will do more on-line training in future
   We will be doing ...

3 not finish / report / by / end of next week
   I will not have finished the report by the end of next week. ✓

4 not use / any paper invoices / next year
   Next year we will not use any paper invoices.
   be using

5 complete / website / by July
   I will have completed the website by July ✓

6 rethink / Internet strategy / over next few weeks
   We will be rethinking our Internet strategy over the next few weeks

7 Internet usage / double / within 5 years
   The Internet usage will doubled within 5 years
   have

8 not launch / products / until / website / complete
   We will not launch any products until our website will have been completed
   has been

Listening Test Part One

- You will hear the Managing Director of a cosmetics manufacturer addressing a group of visitors about the history of the company.
- As you listen, for questions **1 - 12**, complete the notes using up to **three** words or a number.
- You will hear the recording twice.

The History of Eldertree Cosmetics

Early days

1   The company was established in _____ by Olivia Jenkins.

2   Her products sold well because of the _____ of natural products.

3   In order to satisfy demand, the owners had to find _____ in 1977.

The 1980s

4   The introduction of new products resulted in the _____ of the business.

5   By recruiting professional expertise, the company managed to secure _____ with major UK retailers.

6   To support further growth, Eldertree needed both the _____ of a bigger company.

7   In 1987 the company was acquired by Greenaway, the UK's largest _____ .

8   To improve productivity, Greenaway decided to build a _____ in 1988.

9   Greenaway also decided to keep Eldertree's _____ for its products.

Eldertree Cosmetics today

10   Greenaway has centralised functions such as its _____ .

11   In spite of its increased size, the company has kept a _____ .

12   In the last decade Eldertree has become a _____ both at home and abroad.

Listening Test Part Two

- You will hear five different people talking about training courses.
- For each extract there are two tasks. For Task One, choose the course each speaker attended from the list **A - H**. For Task Two, choose the complaint each speaker makes about the course from the list **I - P**.
- You will hear the recording twice.

TASK ONE - TRAINING COURSE

- For questions **13 - 17**, match the extracts with the training course attended, listed **A - H**.
- For each extract, choose the training course attended.
- Write **one** letter **A - H** next to the number of the extract.

13 .....

14 .....

15 .....

A	telephoning skills
B	presentation skills
C	time-management skills
D	team-leadership skills
E	assertiveness skills
F	negotiating skills
G	meeting skills
H	writing skills

16 .....

17 .....

TASK TWO - COMPLAINT

- For questions **18 - 22**, match the extracts with the complaints, listed **I - P**.
- For each extract, choose the speaker's main complaint about the course.
- Write **one** letter **I - P** next to the number of the extract.

18 .....

19 .....

20 .....

21 .....

22 .....

I	the course cost too much
J	the food was disappointing
K	the centre was too far away
L	the course was too short
M	the trainer was disorganised
N	the course went on for too long
O	the group was too big
P	the course started late

Listening Test Part Three

- You will hear an interview with the manager of a corporate travel agency.
- For each question **23 - 30**, mark **one** letter **A**, **B** or **C** for the correct answer.
- You will hear the recording twice.

23 The main effect of winning the award has been the increase in

    A staff motivation.

    B media publicity.

    C new business.

24 Why did Peter start *Corporate Direct*?

    A His local travel agencies had no vacancies.

    B His wife wanted him to work from home.

    C His ambition was to be self-employed.

25 Which *Corporate Direct* service is expanding most rapidly?

    A the car rental scheme

    B the company magazine

    C the currency exchange service

26 Why is *Corporate Direct* unique in the South-East?

    A It is an independent travel agency.

    B It holds detailed client information.

    C It offers the most competitive rates.

27 Which consultancy service is the most popular?

    A language training

    B travel insurance

    C business entertaining

28 Why do companies use a corporate travel agency?

    A It saves them valuable time.

    B It guarantees service standards.

    C It offers the best available prices.

29 *Corporate Direct's* biggest clients are

    A financial service companies.

    B hotel and catering firms.

    C fashion retailers.

30 Which new service will be available to clients next?

    A an on-line reservation system

    B a new company credit card

    C a 24-hour telephone helpline

Reading Test Part Four

- Read the terms and conditions of employment below.
- Choose the best word to fill each gap.
- For each question **1 - 10**, mark **one** letter **A**, **B**, **C** or **D**.
- There is an example at the beginning **(0)**.

Terms and Conditions of Employment

The employee works a $37^1/_2$ hour week, which includes some evening work. The salary is based on Key Scale 3, with a **(0)** ..A.. for shift work. Weekday overtime is paid at a standard hourly **(1)** ..C.. , which increases to double-time at weekends. The employee's **(2)** C..2.' are as detailed in the attached letter of employment.

The salary is calculated from 25th - 24th inclusive of each month and is **(3)** ..D.. to the employee's bank account on the last day of the month, except where the last day of the month falls on a weekend, in which case it is paid on the previous Friday.

The company's holiday year runs from April 1st each year. The employee is **(4)** ..D.. to two days' paid holiday per month worked, with three extra days' holiday during the Christmas period. All holidays must be taken within the holiday year (1st April - 31st March). Those not taken by 31st March may not be **(5)** ..... over to the following year. All holiday dates are **(6)** ..... to management approval.

During the first four months of employment, the employee is on a period of **(7)** ..... . Within this period, employment may be **(8)** ..... by either party provided that at least one week's **(9)** ..... is given in writing.

The age of **(10)** ..... for all employees is 65. However, an employee may be allowed to work beyond this age, provided that the employment contract is renewed annually. The company does not operate a private pension scheme for employees.

Example

0 A bonus   B premium   C benefit   D prize

A   B   C   D
■   ☐   ☐   ☐

1	A charge	B rate	C fare	D tariff
2	A jobs	B routines	C duties	D tasks
3	A diverted	B accounted	C dispatched	D credited
4	A entitled	B authorised	C entrusted	D admitted
5	A passed	B taken	C carried	D put
6	A subject	B exposed	C subordinate	D referred
7	A appraisal	B placement	C analysis	D probation
8	A terminated	B destroyed	C eliminated	D abolished
9	A caution	B notice	C instruction	D advice
10	A removal	B release	C retirement	D resignation

The Reading Test

Overview

The Reading Test has six parts testing various reading skills. Part Four specifically tests a candidate's knowledge of vocabulary.

Part	Input	Task
1	Five 90 word texts	Matching sentences with texts
2	450-500 word text	Sentence level gap-filling
3	500-600 word text	Multiple-choice comprehension questions
4	250 word text	Single word multiple-choice gap-filling
5	250 word text	Single word gap-filling
6	150-200 word text	Proof-reading: identifying extra words

Length: 60 minutes

How to succeed

Here are some important general tips for doing the Reading Test.

- Read all instructions **carefully**.
- Begin with the part of the Reading Test you feel most confident about. You do not need to do the parts of the test in order.
- Leave difficult questions and return to them later if you have time.
- **Never** leave a question unanswered. If you run out of time or have no idea, guess.
- Leave enough time to do all the Writing Test. It represents 27 per cent of the final mark.
- Read through the whole text once before looking at the questions.
- The questions are generally in the same order as the answers. If you are confident that an answer is correct, begin reading for the next answer from that point, not from the beginning.
- Underline the answers in the text - it will make checking quicker.
- Only write **one** answer for each question.
- Use any time you have left to check your answers.

The reading tasks

1 Part One tests the ability to read for both gist and specific information. Read the text and the three sentences below. Which sentence matches the text best? Underline the parts of the text which help you to identify the correct option.

A   *Business Strategies for the Internet*

What opportunities does the Internet offer your business? Can it make significant cost savings? Can it reshape your entire supply chain? *Business Strategies for the Internet* uses basic business principles to show how businesses can make best use of the Internet. The authors argue that imagination and lateral thinking, not technical know-how, are the key sources of competitive advantage. They demonstrate why much corporate investment in the Internet has been unsuccessful and show how failures could have been avoided. More than 100 case studies are analysed, showing how the Internet's strengths have been successfully exploited. The authors are senior partners in *Net Gains*, one of the country's leading consultancies on the commercial exploitation of Web-based technology.

---

1 The authors demonstrate the importance of specialised technical skills.
2 The book shows how to cut distribution costs dramatically.
3 Real-life examples are used in the book to illustrate good practice.

Exam tips: Reading Test Part One
- The correct sentence will not normally use exactly the same words as the text.
- Words from the other, incorrect, sentences might appear in the text.
- Each text will normally be used at least once.
- Decide which is the best technique for you: reading each text first and then all the options, or reading each option first and then all five texts.

❷ Part Two tests the ability to ensure that the overall meaning of a text is clear and that ideas are logically ordered and linked. Read the extract and the three sentences below. Which sentence fills the gap best? Why do the other sentences not fit?

are still faced by the question 'Will staff actually want to relocate?'.

To assume that staff will automatically relocate in order to keep their jobs is a mistake. They may have family commitments or regard the destination as undesirable. Staff that are being considered for relocation are probably valuable and could find another job locally. [**10**] This might not be cheap, but neither is losing key staff that the company has invested in over several years. The company needs to weigh up the attractiveness of

A It makes sense then to consult staff when choosing a destination for relocation.
B Therefore, a company needs to offer a package that will persuade them to move.
C By providing practical help, a company can minimise these difficulties.

Exam tips: Reading Test Part Two
- Read at least one sentence either side of each gap before filling it.
- Ensure that each sentence fits the gap grammatically.
- Pay special attention to linking words, reference words and pronouns.
- Check each sentence fits in with the logic of the text as a whole.
- Read the completed text to check your answers. Does it feel right?

❸ Part Three tests the ability to read for specific information. Read the extract and the question below. Which option answers the question best?

Call centre technology has enabled companies to revolutionise their activities. Services such as freefone product information hotlines or the telephone-based distribution networks of companies like Direct Line Insurance are now cost-effective and easy to implement. Although sales may also be involved, with airlines, for example, using centralised reservations offices, call centres are not about telemarketing techniques such as cold calling consumers in the middle of their dinner to sell them double-glazing; they are a response to the fact that consumers now expect quick access to information when it suits them and not the company.

I Why have call centres become so popular?
A More and more people are buying products over the phone.
B They are a cheap way for a company to distribute its goods.
C People now expect fast and convenient customer service.
D Freefone services are a successful marketing technique.

Exam tips: Reading Test Part Three
- Scan the text to find the relevant passage and read it carefully.
- Be careful of options that use the same words as in the text.
- Base all answers on information printed in the text - not world knowledge.
- Choose only one answer for each question.

4 Part Four tests vocabulary. Candidates complete a text by choosing one of four options to fill each gap. Before looking at the options on the next page, underline the words around each gap indicating the type of word missing. Think of a word for each gap.

Calgary Plastics has a policy of actively promoting the development of its staff. This is achieved in a range of ways throughout the company including induction courses, in-service training, training weekends, external training and appraisals.

We believe that this personal and professional development is of **(1)** ..... to both the company and individual employees. It enables the company to retain high-calibre, **(2)** ..... staff and thus offer a better product to our customers. It also provides us with a **(3)** ..... of able people with relevant experience for the management positions which inevitably **(4)** ..... within a large company such as Calgary Plastics.

Our focus on staff development and our policy of internal recruitment where possible mean that skilled employees have the opportunity to **(5)** ..... their careers rapidly within a framework which offers the necessary training to help them **(6)** ..... effectively in more senior positions.

This booklet is intended to assist us in **(7)** ..... your development by providing an easily accessible record of your training and professional development to date. It also **(8)** ..... appraisal procedures and gives advice on how to prepare for appraisal interviews.

Please try to ensure that you **(9)** ..... your records up to date and present your training portfolio at appraisal interviews so that your line manager or department head will be able to **(10)** ..... your future development needs.

Exam tips: Reading Test Part Four
- Read the whole text first to get a feel for the context and style.
- Use the words around each gap to predict the word missing.
- All the options are grammatically possible but only one is correct.
- Read the completed text to check your answers. Does it feel right?

5 Now choose the best word to fill each gap in the text on the previous page.

		A	B	C	D
1		A profit	B credit	C benefit	D merit
2		A committed	B engaged	C contracted	D pledged
3		A fund	B pool	C collection	D store
4		A present	B arise	C happen	D develop
5		A progress	B elevate	C advance	D raise
6		A function	B serve	C practise	D officiate
7		A proving	B testing	C controlling	D monitoring
8		A outlines	B portrays	C represents	D displays
9		A maintain	B keep	C retain	D hold
10		A guess	B value	C assess	D rate

6 Part Five tests grammar and understanding of cohesion. Candidates complete a gapped text with suitable words. No options are given. Underline the words around each gap which help you identify the missing word. Now fill the gaps.

Female entrepreneurs as successful as men

A report published this week by WestLink Small Business Services shows that women are still **(1)** ..... likely to start new business ventures than men, although they are usually better qualified and more realistic in their business planning. The report found **(2)** ..... women were responsible for only 30 per cent of the 232,000 UK start-ups in the first half of 1999. Moreover, there has been little change in the proportion of male to female start-ups over the last 13 years **(3)** ..... the growth in women-owned businesses in areas such as nannying, fitness training, gardening and interior design.

Few banks are addressing this issue. A WestLink spokesman, **(4)** ....., would like to see more women starting their own business ventures: 'Studies have shown that gender has **(5)** ..... effect whatsoever on the potential success of a business. The crucial factors are age, vocational qualifications, amount of relevant experience and the number of people employed by the start-up business.'

Most businesses started by women tend to be in certain industries **(6)** ..... as domestic and professional services, catering and leisure. This might be explained by the fact that these areas typically offer more flexible working patterns, **(7)** ..... is a major factor for working women with families.

One distinct difference **(8)** ..... male and female entrepreneurs concerns the level of first year turnover predicted in their business plans. Men, on average, forecast a first year turnover of £150,000 **(9)** ..... women hoped to make a more modest £74,000 on their first year's trading. The report showed that the lower figure represented a more realistic approach **(10)** ..... than lower expectations.

Exam tips: Reading Test Part Five
- Read the whole text first to get a feel for the context and style.
- Read at least one sentence either side of each gap before filling it.
- Fill each gap with only one word.
- Read the completed text to check the grammar is correct. Is the overall meaning clear?

7 Part Six tests proof-reading ability. Candidates identify any extra words in the numbered lines of a short text. Some lines are correct. Read the following text and underline the incorrect words. Why are they incorrect?

Language skills in business

0	In today's global markets, businesses have to communicate internationally
00	and every language barriers have to be overcome. That's the reason why
1	people with good language skills they are needed by international
2	businesses order to negotiate with customers, deal with suppliers,
3	contribute to meetings and manage overseas subsidiaries. One of the best
4	ways to deal with such a varied language needs is through well-planned and
5	relevant language learning programmes. An individual training programme
6	which can focus on the precise language skills people need to do their job
7	properly and help them to achieve their learning objectives appropriately.
8	Developing language skills takes time but the effective communication is
9	crucial in today's international markets.

Exam tips: Reading Test Part Six

- Read the whole text first to get a feel for the context and style.
- Underline any words which seem strange.
- Concentrate on small grammatical words such as articles, pronouns and prepositions.
- Make sure you have no more than one mistake on any single line.
- Read the whole sentence to check whether your answer is correct.
- Read the completed text to check your answers. Does it feel right?

The Listening Test

Overview

The Listening Test has three parts.

Part	Input	Task
I	3-4 minute monologue	Gap-filling (words and numbers)
2	5 short monologues	Matching monologues with topics/places etc. Matching the same monologues with functions, attitudes, opinions etc.
3	4-5 minute conversation	Multiple-choice comprehension questions

Length: A total of 15 minutes of listening material played twice, plus 10 minutes at the end to transfer answers to the Answer Sheet.

Before listening

It is important that you use your time well **before** you listen. Here are some tips.

- Read the instructions **very carefully** before you listen.
- Check the type of answer you need to give.
- You will always be given time to read through the questions before you listen. Use this time well. Try to predict what you might hear and what the answers might be.

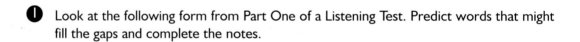 Look at the following form from Part One of a Listening Test. Predict words that might fill the gaps and complete the notes.

PART ONE
- You will hear a company representative outlining the programme of a sales conference.
- As you listen, for questions **1 - 12**, complete the notes using up to **three** words or a number.
- You will hear the recording twice.

Annual Sales Conference

The programme

1 9.30 The conference will begin with .... in the main foyer.
2 10.00 This will be followed by a report on .... by Nigel Laws, Group MD.
3 11.30 There will be a short break for .... before the first workshop.

While listening

1 Look at the following Part Three question and the tapescript below. Why might some candidates choose a wrong option?

2 The company dramatically improved its profits by
   A cutting production costs.
   B developing new products.
   C reducing product prices.

	needed to improve margins.
Interviewer	So just how did you manage to improve profits so dramatically?
Annette	Well, first of all, we looked at ways of cutting production costs and the possibility of a large advertising campaign to re-launch existing brands. But in the end we decided to revamp our lines - several people at the time wanted to win market share back by aggressive discounting but we were confident that our designers could win back customers with fresh, exciting ideas. It meant a lot of investment, but it's paid off.

Interviewer It certainly has. What in...

After listening

1 Always check your answers very carefully. Look at the question papers below. Find the candidate's mistakes.

PART ONE
- You will hear a PR Manager talking about a forthcoming press launch.
- As you listen, for questions **1 - 12**, complete the notes using up to **three** words or a number.
- You will hear the recording twice.

XR300 Press Launch

The programme

1 9.30 Welcome speech by Tom Watts, who is the Director of Axon UK.

PART TWO: TASK ONE
- You will hear five different people talking about their jobs.
- For each extract there are two tasks. For Task One, choose the job title of each speaker from the list **A - H**.
- You will hear the recording twice.

13 A/B.
14 ...A...

A	Secretary
B	Accountant
C	Receptionist

PART THREE
- You will hear an interview with the manager of a large retailer.
- For each question **23 - 30**, mark **one** letter A, B or C for the correct answer.
- You will hear the recording twice.

23 The company is looking to expand in order to
   (A) increase its profit margins.
   B extend its range of products.
   (C) break into foreign markets.

The Writing Test

Overview

The Writing Test has two parts.

Part	Input	Task
1	Instructions and graph	Writing a short description of a graph (120-140 words)
2	Instructions	Writing a letter, short report or proposal (200-250 words)

Length: 70 minutes

How to succeed

The Writing Test assesses performance in several areas: task completion, organisation and linking of ideas, appropriateness, range and accuracy of vocabulary and grammar.

Task
- Successful task completion means fulfilling all parts of the task. Full marks can be awarded only when all the points in the rubric are covered fully and appropriately.
- Keep to the word limit. If you are below it, you have probably not fully completed the task. If you are above it, you have probably included unnecessary information.

Language
- Show a range of grammar and vocabulary.
- Organise and link your ideas clearly.
- Use language which is consistent and appropriate.
- Check your writing **carefully** when you have finished.

Describing graphs

1 Part One tests the ability to describe a graph. Look at the following task and the sample answer below. Does the answer fulfil the task?

PART ONE
- The graph below shows sales for two companies between 1995 - 1999.
- Using information from the graph, write a short **report** describing and comparing the performance of the two companies during this period.
- Write **120 - 140** words on your Answer Sheet.

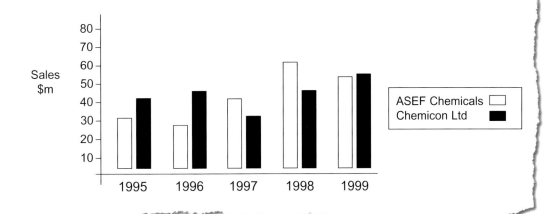

Exam tip:
You have little time and only a few words, so describe general trends. Don't just give a long list of detailed, individual movements.

In 1995 ASEF Chemicals made sales of just a little bit over $30m and then in the following year, which was 1996, the sales at ASEF Chemicals went down to about the $25m level. The next year, however, sales went up very quickly and ASEF Chemicals made slightly over $40m but the next year sales went up even more quickly than they did the year before and they reached $60m in 1998. But then, in 1999, the sales dropped just a little bit and ASEF Chemicals made sales of about only $50m, which wasn't very good for that company.

Sales at Chemicon Ltd started higher at over $40m, which was about $10m more than at ASEF Chemicals but they only went up a little bit the following year to about the $45m level. But then sales at Chemicon Ltd fell very much and were only at $30m, which was a lot less than ASEF Chemicals. But in both the next year, which was 1998, and in 1999 they went back up again and the sales achieved a bit over $50m by the end of 1999, which was just a little bit more than ASEF Chemicals.

2 Consider how the following affect the conciseness of the sample answer.

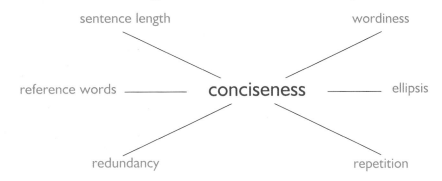

How else can the sample answer be improved? Rewrite it in 120-140 words.

Report writing

① In Part Two candidates may be asked to write a short report. Read the following task and the sample answer below. Does the answer fulfil the task?

PART TWO
- Your company has decided to invest some of this year's exceptionally high profits in one of the following areas:
  - New computers
  - Language training courses
  - Special bonus payments.
- You have been asked to write a **report** recommending how the profits should be invested and what benefits would be achieved.
- Write **200 - 250** words on your Answer Sheet.

This report is about how the company should invest some of this year's exceptionally high profits into one of the following areas - New Computers, Language Training Courses, Special Bonus Payments. First of all new computers. Most employees have computers which are fast enough to handle the work which they normally do on them. These computers are not very old. The company wants to increase its export sales. This is especially in Spain and France. Language training courses would be a very good idea for all the staff who have to speak with business partners and customers in these countries.

The staff would enjoy the lessons and feel that the company is investing in them. Moreover, it is good for motivation. Furthermore, special bonus is also good for motivation however does not invest anything in the company. The staff might expect to get such bonus every time the company makes good profits and then there might be some problems. It is not recommended. Finally, who do you give the special bonus to? It can cause problems. I think it would be the best if the company invests the high profits in language training because that is the best for both the staff and the company. The courses should be for anyone who has contact with partners and customers.

2 What main points do you think the writer is trying to make? What reasons does he/she give in support of these main points?

Main points	Supporting ideas

3 Is the sample answer organised in logical paragraphs? How many paragraphs does the report need?

4 Rewrite the sample answer to make the writer's original ideas easier to understand. Consider the following.

paragraphing   layout (headings, bullets etc.)

organisation
of reports

main points and supporting ideas   linking words and phrases

5 Look at the Writing Test Assessment Sheet on page 71. Consider the questions and make any necessary changes to your report.

Formal letter writing

1 Alternatively, candidates may be asked to write a formal letter in Part Two. Read the following task and a candidate's handwritten notes below.

PART TWO
- A foreign business associate is visiting your company for three days. You have been asked to organise the visit and plan appropriate entertainment.
- Write a **letter** to the visitor outlining a timetable for the visit and describing the activities you have planned.
- Write **200 - 250** words on your Answer Sheet.

Thursday
Pick Ricardo up at 10.15 from the airport
Take him to hotel and check in
Business lunch & then to company for meeting
Dinner at Ricardo's hotel - time to be arranged

Friday
Meeting at company 9.30
Working lunch - get sandwiches delivered
Meeting until about 17.00
Give Ricardo time to freshen up
Dinner at The Riverside Lodge restaurant 20.00

Saturday
Ricardo in company golf tournament - tee off at 8.30
Formal dinner with speaker at golf club 19.30

Sunday
Return flight to Madrid 09.45

Now use the candidate's notes to write the letter. Consider the following.

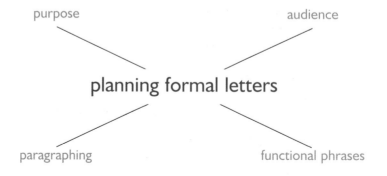

purpose   audience

planning formal letters

paragraphing   functional phrases

2 Look at the Writing Test Assessment Sheet on page 71. Consider the questions and make any necessary changes to your letter.

Essential report writing phrases

Introduction
This report aims/sets out to ...
The aim/purpose of this report is to ...
The report is based on ...

Findings
It was found that ...
The following points summarise our key findings.
The key findings are outlined below.

Conclusion (s)
It was decided/agreed/felt that ...
It is clear that ...
No conclusions were reached regarding ...

Recommendation (s)
It is suggested/proposed/recommended that ...
We (strongly) recommend that ...
It is essential to ...
It would be advisable to ...

Signalling
The following areas of concern have been highlighted.
There are a number of reasons for ...
There are several factors which affect ...
A further factor is ...
This raises a number of issues.
As might have been expected, ...
Contrary to expectations, ...

Essential letter writing phrases

Referring to previous contact
Thank you for your interest ...
With reference to your letter of/dated ... in which ...
Further to our conversation of ...

Stating the reason for writing
I am writing to confirm/apply for/outline ...
I would like to thank/complain/comment on ...
I am writing concerning ...

Enclosing information
Please find enclosed ...
As requested, I enclose ...

Offering assistance
Should you have any further questions, please contact me on the above number.
In the meantime, if you require any further information, please do not hesitate to call me.

Referring to future contact
I look forward to hearing from you/meeting you/seeing you/working with you.
I hope to hear from you soon.

Writing Test Assessment Sheet

TASK	Are all the points in the rubric adequately covered?	
	Is the answer the correct length?	

ORGANISATION	Is it easy to follow the writer's ideas?	
	Are the writer's main points adequately supported?	
	Is the layout clear and appropriate? (paragraphs, headings, bullets etc.)	

CLARITY	Is the answer free of redundancy and repetition?	
	Are the sentences of an appropriate length?	
	Are linking words and phrases used clearly and naturally?	

LANGUAGE	Is there a range of vocabulary, grammar and functional language?	
	Is the language generally accurate?	
	Is the formality and tone appropriate and consistent?	

COMMENTS	

The Speaking Test

Overview

The Speaking Test takes place with two, or possibly three, candidates and two examiners. The first examiner speaks to the candidates. The second examiner listens and assesses the candidates' English.

Part	Format	Input	Task
1	Examiner talks to each candidate individually	Examiner asks questions	Speaking about yourself Responding to questions
2	Candidate talks to candidate	Written prompt	Giving a one-minute talk
3	Candidates discuss a topic together	Written prompt	Completing a collaborative task

How to succeed

The Speaking Test assesses performance in a number of areas. Here are some important tips for each area.

Interactive communication
- Listen **carefully** to all instructions.
- Ask the examiner to repeat any instructions you are not sure about.
- Give full appropriate answers, not just one or two words.
- Keep to and complete the task. Do not talk about other things.
- Good communication means working with and not competing with the other candidate.

Organisation of ideas
Consider the following:
- your main points
- your supporting ideas
- how to order and link your ideas.

Grammar and vocabulary
- You will be marked on both the range and accuracy of your grammar and vocabulary. You therefore need to demonstrate variety in your language. However, if you try to be too ambitious, you risk being penalised for lack of accuracy.

Pronunciation
- Speak clearly and at a natural speed.

Personal information

❶ In Part One of the Speaking Test the examiner will ask the candidates some general questions about themselves. Work in pairs. Your teacher will give you some cards. Take a card and ask your partner about the topic on the card.

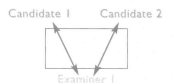

Exam tips: Speaking Test Part One
- Ask the examiner to clarify if you do not fully understand a question.
- Answer each question fully and keep to the question.
- Speak to the examiner and not the other candidate in Part One.
- Do not interrupt the other candidate in this part of the test.

Short talk

❶ In Part Two of the Speaking Test each candidate talks for one minute on one of three given topics. Candidates are given a minute to prepare their ideas. Look at the following topics. Which would you choose to talk about? Why?

Business Travel:	The importance of a good hotel when travelling on business
Sales:	How to provide good customer service
Marketing:	The importance of good product positioning

❷ Listen to Natacha and Salvatore giving their talks. Use the Speaking Test Assessment Sheet on page 76 to assess their performance.

3 Now listen to Natacha and Salvatore doing the task again. In what way is their performance better?

4 Following each short talk, the other candidate is expected to ask a relevant question. What questions would you ask Natacha and Salvatore?

5 Use the framework below to plan a one-minute talk on one of the following topics.

Exam tip:
Use your preparation time well. List and order your main points and supporting ideas.

Communication:	How to ensure good communication within teams
Personnel:	The importance of providing staff training
Finance:	How to raise capital for new investment

Opening sentence: _____

_____

Main points

• _____

• _____

• _____

Supporting ideas

• _____

• _____

• _____

Concluding sentence: _____

_____

6 Now work in pairs. Take turns to give your talk. Use the Speaking Test Assessment Sheet on page 76 to assess your partner's performance.

Collaborative task

❶ Part Three tests the ability to discuss a given issue and reach certain decisions. Look at the following task and the Speaking Test Assessment Sheet on the opposite page. Then listen to Natacha and Salvatore and assess their performance.

> Your company is entertaining foreign visitors for three days. You have been asked to organise social activities for them. Discuss and decide together:
>
> - which company representatives the guests should meet
> - what activities would be suitable.

Exam tips: Speaking Test Part Three
- Read the task instructions very carefully.
- Use the preparation time given to organise your ideas.
- Begin by quickly agreeing on a context (the type of company you work for etc.).
- Give reasons to support your ideas.
- Invite your partner to express his/her ideas and respond to them.
- When you disagree, say why and give an alternative idea.
- Make sure you are moving the task towards a conclusion.
- Recap and summarise your decisions when necessary.

❷ Now listen to Natacha and Salvatore doing the same task again. In what way is their performance better?

Candidate 1 ◄──► Candidate 2

Examiner 1

Examiner 2

❸ Work in pairs. Do the following task.

> Your company is launching a new product. You have been asked to organise a public relations event as part of the launch. Discuss and decide together:
>
> - who should be invited
> - what the programme should involve.

Speaking Test Assessment Sheet

		Student A	Student B
SHORT TALK	Does the student show a clear understanding of the task?		
	Is there an appropriate introduction and conclusion?		
	Are the student's ideas well-organised and logically ordered?		
	Is appropriate signposting and linking language used?		
	Does the student develop ideas rather than repeat them?		
	Are the ideas clearly expressed and easy to understand?		
	Does the student speak in a clear and natural manner?		
	Is the talk of an appropriate length?		

COMMENTS

		Student A	Student B
COLLABORATIVE TASK	Does the student show a clear understanding of the task?		
	Is there an attempt to establish a shared context?		
	Does the student give reasons to support opinions?		
	Does the student listen and respond to other opinions?		
	Are the student's ideas easy to understand?		
	Does the student ask for clarification when necessary?		
	Does the student agree and disagree appropriately and naturally?		
	Does the student summarise and move the task towards a conclusion?		

COMMENTS

Staff motivation

What motivates staff?

Speaking ❶ Read the following statements. Do you agree? Why/Why not?

- Managers assume that the goals of employees are those of the company.
- Motivation stems from job satisfaction and not financial reward.

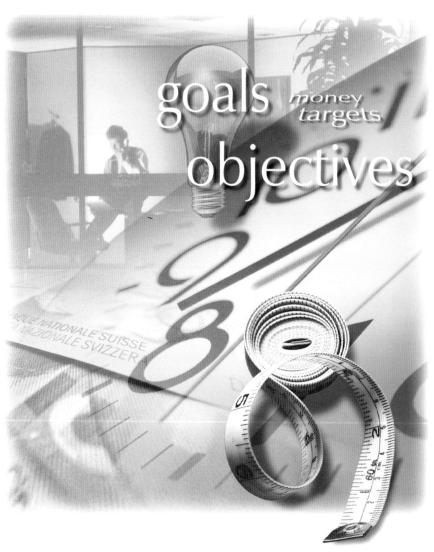

Reading ❷ Read the newspaper article on the opposite page. What is the writer's attitude to motivational techniques? Do you share this attitude?

Meeting the company's motivational challenge

Adrian Furnham *discusses the thorny issue of putting motivational techniques into practice.*

[handwritten: Do you know any?]

Managers, company owners and supervisors have always been frustrated and bewildered by employees with little or no motivation.

We have all seen the 'quit-but-stay' employees who have severed their psychological contact with the organisation. Nothing seems to fire them up. They firmly park their brains and their enthusiasm for life in the staff car park in the morning, re-engaging them with gusto 30 seconds after the official end of work time.

[handwritten: How does this make you feel?]

However, they shrewdly avoid doing anything that warrants dismissal and are content to keep their heads down, doing the minimum and volunteering nothing. This leaves the company with little option other than to mark them down as candidates for the next round of redundancies.

But what management techniques are available to repair and restore motivation?

☑ Give employees as much meaningful work as possible. The less intrinsically interesting the work, the more needs to be done to make it acceptable: job enrichment, job rotation and job sharing.

☑ Give employees the information and resources needed to do a good job. Also ensure, through ongoing training, that employees have the necessary skills to meet the requirements of the job.

☑ Demonstrate a commitment to career development and promotion from within.

☑ Foster a sense of team spirit. You do not have to organise outdoor assault courses. It is enough to provide opportunities for people to meet, talk and share together.

☑ Publicly recognise and congratulate employees for good work. Celebrate success; create heroes.

☑ Provide regular and specific feedback to all staff through both formal appraisals and informal channels of communication. Encourage feedback from staff and involve employees in decisions that affect their work.

☑ Pay people what they are worth. Consider such factors as market forces, predatory competitors and the contribution each individual makes.

[handwritten: What's popular today?]

The astute reader may be tempted to ask: so what is really new? The answer is: nothing really.

[handwritten: Trend]

Ideas in motivation get repackaged, renamed and rebranded, but fundamentally remain the same as ever. Fads and fashions in the management consultancy world seem to dictate which particular technique is seen as the most powerful and popular at any given time.

The fact that we know some of the key factors in motivation, however, has not prevented many managers from ignoring them. Some people are fortunate enough to have a good boss, who may have modelled positive motivational behaviours. But because few managers are trained or educated in the art of motivation and have themselves never been well-managed, we get the perpetuation of incompetence.

[handwritten: Do you know any such bosses?]

This explains the paradox of why people have heard about but not seen successful motivational management in practice.

[handwritten: Which techniques do you think are most effective?]

Adapted from the **Sunday Telegraph**, October 25 1998

Speaking ❸ Read the article again and discuss the handwritten questions.

A motivation survey

Listening ❶   Terrain Ltd, a leisurewear manufacturer, is investigating staff motivation. Listen to five employees talking to the HR Manager. Which grievance does each speaker refer to?

1 .....

2 .....

3 .....

4 .....

5 .....

A   too much responsibility

B   uninteresting work   4

C   lack of communication   5

D   uncooperative colleagues

E   lack of recognition   3

F   unsatisfactory pay   2

G   inflexible working hours

H   lack of clear objectives   1

Language ❷   Look at the HR Manager's incomplete report on staff motivation on the opposite page. Underline examples of the following features.

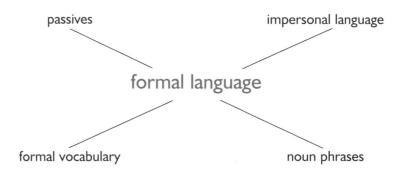

passives   impersonal language

formal language

formal vocabulary   noun phrases

3 Complete the *Findings* section of the report by summarising the grievances of the Terrain employees.   Page 134

Report on Staff   Motivation

Introduction

This report presents the results of the recent survey of staff motivation. The findings are based on interviews with employees from all departments within the company.

Findings

Conclusion

It is clear that there are significant levels of dissatisfaction regarding certain issues within the company. Unless these issues are addressed as a matter of urgency, the consequent demotivation of staff will undoubtedly have a negative impact on the performance of the company.

Recommendations

Ellough Industrial Estate ➤ BECCLES ➡ Suffolk ❀ NR34 7RY ✈ Tel 01502 714281 ✦ Fax 01502 714282 ❀

4 What recommendations would you make to address the grievances? Use your ideas to complete the report.

Optional task **5** Design a questionnaire to find what motivates your fellow students in English lessons.

Recruitment

Recruitment methods

Speaking ❶ What are the advantages and disadvantages of the following?

- internal recruitment
- job advertisements
- recruitment agencies
- headhunting

...d was keen to install a candidate for the new position as a delay in

...il be headed by R Stevens, who will lead the new Finance Division of the company.

...ccept-corporations. ...with the new ...e in place it ...s unlikely that the ...CEO will be capa- ...of maintaining such ...trict control over the ...ompany's recruitment ...policy, which, up until now, has dictated the type of candidates that

HEAD HUNTERS plc

So - How did you get on with your first day in the field?

Cartoon by Colin Wheeler

Reading ❷ Read the first two paragraphs of the article on the opposite page. Match the sentences in italics with the following functions.

| explaining | comparing | emphasising | contrasting | exemplifying |

❸ Now complete the article by choosing the best sentence to fill each gap.

A They are the currency by which headhunting operates.

B If, for example, the original contact is unavailable, a colleague will answer the phone and happily divulge their own name.

C All of these conversations with the headhunter will be handled discreetly to save any embarrassment at work.

D A team of researchers will have done some initial searching and compiled a list of suitable candidates.

E With clever questioning, the headhunter can navigate around the rest of the department and quickly compile a list of names and likely job roles.

F Anyone contributing to an on-line newsgroup with informed, specialist opinion may well become the target of a headhunter.

So why do people headhunt?

'The reason headhunting works is because we target the individual,' says Adelaide Macaulay of London-based Morgan Howard International. 'If a company needs to fill a niche role in a niche market, then they'll come to us.' Macaulay recruits for a number of clients spread throughout Europe. Each company needs to fill an important or highly-specialised role and thinks traditional advertising would not be effective. *This is particularly the case as 99 per cent of the people Macaulay targets are not actively on the market.* She usually targets people who are happy in their job and not looking to move. However, an Achilles heel can usually be found that allows the headhunter to persuade them that they are, in fact, wanting to change. *It may be that they are fed up with the company, that they want more money, or that they want a change of location.*

Internet headhunting firm Netsearch is more blunt than Macaulay about the reason why companies turn to headhunters: 'Headhunting is relatively cheap and on the increase as selection gets worse and worse.' Recruiters divide their business into 'selection' and 'search' processes. *The former category refers to traditional advertising and the latter to the activities of the headhunter.* Recruitment officers believe that for certain vacancies advertising is too expensive and throws up hundreds of largely unsuitable CVs, which take hours to process. *Headhunters, on the other hand, have enough tricks up their sleeve to produce a shorter, better quality list of candidates.* With search, they insist, you can get a better person more quickly.

Headhunters are understandably unwilling to reveal their methods. However, one source did claim that if he had one name and extension number, within a matter of hours he would have a good idea of who everyone in the department is and what they do. ⬚1⬚ By a simple process of deduction, it is then easy to work out that person's position in the company; if people are sitting at adjacent desks, the chances are that they are in similar roles. ⬚2⬚ This information can then be stored for future reference.

One thing all of this makes clear is the importance of names. ⬚3⬚ Any name a headhunter comes across is written down and put on record. This process has been made much easier with the invention of e-mail, which indicates a person's name, employer and even the department they work in. ⬚4⬚ Companies like Netsearch constantly monitor such forums hunting for potential candidates.

Adapted from the www.taps.com website, June 1999

4 Underline the reference words and phrases in the text. Which refer to a passage of text and not to a single noun?

Speaking **5** A key staff member has just left your company and you have been asked to recruit a replacement. Discuss and decide the following.

- ◎ the qualities required for the job
- ◎ the best method of recruiting a replacement

Listening ❶ Guy Kirkwood specialises in executive search in the IT sector. Listen to his presentation about headhunting and complete the notes using up to three words or a number.

Headhunting

A presentation by Guy Kirkwood from the executive search firm antiphon

◎ Introduction

1 The UK recruitment market is divided into four categories: _____ , advertising selection, a combination of the two and executive search.

2 The headhunting market is expanding due to _____ within specific markets, especially in the finance, consulting and information technology sectors.

◎ The headhunting process

3 The headhunter begins by identifying possible candidates through _____ or extensive contact networks.

4 After making contact, the headhunter interviews candidates at their company offices or at a _____ .

5 The headhunter then collates candidates' CVs and _____ to the client, who shortlists three or four candidates.

6 The client then interviews the candidates, after which the headhunter provides feedback and assists in the _____ to ensure a successful conclusion.

◎ Fees

7 The headhunter will charge a percentage of the appointee's _____ .

8 The fee is normally charged as _____ , a shortlist fee and a completion fee.

◎ The advantages of headhunting

9 Headhunters offer knowledge of the market, their client's business, their _____ and those of their competitors.

10 This is achieved through extensive research, contact with the _____ in the market and international exposure.

11 Headhunting saves clients time and gives them access to _____ information.

12 Headhunting identifies people who are professionally satisfied, _____ and highly competent - exactly the type of people who can most benefit the client.

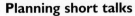

2 Look at the following checklist for planning short talks. Listen to Guy's presentation again. How does he address the following points?

Planning short talks

Remember these points when planning a short talk.

- **Purpose**
  What is the purpose of the talk? (e.g. to explain a procedure)

- **Content**
  What are the main points?
  How are these points supported?

- **Organisation**
  How could you order your main points? (e.g. chronological sequence)
  How could you introduce and conclude your talk?

- **Language**
  What linking words and phrases could you use?
  What other useful phrases could you use?

Speaking **3** Talk about one of the following topics for one minute. Prepare your talk using the questions above.

- how to fill a key vacancy
- the importance of having a good CV

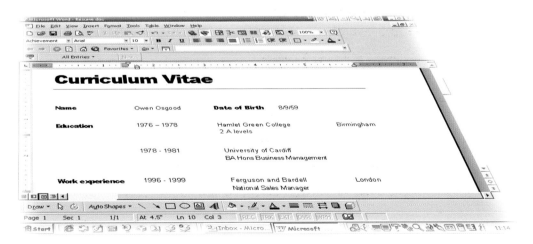

Writing **4** Find a job advertisement and write a 200-250 word letter of application. Include your reasons for applying and explain what you can bring to the job.

1 Some of the following lines contain an unnecessary word. Underline any extra words in lines 1-12.

1 The findings are being based on interviews with ten senior
2 managers and two directors which as well as a
3 questionnaire sent to more than fifty employees at the
4 leisurewear manufacturer's main production facility in
5 Suffolk. It was found that such levels of staff motivation
6 were extremely low throughout of the organisation. In
7 particular, staff expressed any dissatisfaction with their
8 current salary levels and said they felt undervalued by the
9 company. It was also found that those inflexible working
10 hours are a certain major grievance among staff at all
11 levels. Other reasons given for job dissatisfaction included
12 uncooperative colleagues, lack of the clear objectives and
too much responsibility.

2 Add *un, in* or *ir* to each of the following words to form its opposite.

1 effective _____
2 significant _____
3 satisfactory _____
4 regular _____
5 appreciated _____
6 flexible _____
7 responsible _____
8 interesting _____
9 capable _____
10 specific _____

Now use either form of the words to complete the following sentences.

1 We pay competitive salaries because we don't want our people to feel _____ and undervalued.

2 Some managers are _____ of understanding that an employee's goals might not be the company's.

3 You can motivate workers by ensuring that they always have _____ and varied work.

4 I find it a lot easier when I'm working towards _____ objectives and goals.

5 Progress meetings tend to be spontaneous and held at pretty _____ intervals.

6 Any motivational technique will be _____ if the employees are determined not to enjoy their work.

7 All the way through the negotiations both sides remained _____ on the issue of longer hours.

8 Management dismissed the union's behaviour as _____ and unreasonable.

3 Match the verbs with a similar meaning. Then think of a word or phrase to follow each verb.

1 remain   cut
2 restore   stay
3 schedule   resign
4 appreciate   deal with
5 sever   rebrand
6 rename   repair
7 address   value
8 quit   plan

4 Complete each sentence with a suitable preposition.

1 I prefer working on big projects because I like to have something to get my teeth _____ .

2 A lot of the problem stems _____ a personality clash between Helen and her line manager.

3 Attitudes _____ motivational techniques vary substantially within the workforce.

4 In terms of pay and conditions, I don't think we are falling _____ our competitors.

5 There's a lack _____ promotion opportunities.

6 Not working overtime is often seen _____ a failure to show commitment to the company.

Passives

5 Complete the text. Put each verb in brackets into the correct form of the passive.

In order to assess past performance and review pay, all employees (**1** *appraise*) __are appraised__ at least once a year. Pay increases (**2** *award*) _____ on the basis of performance and (**3** *not/base*) _____ on the length of service at the company. Despite the fact that this system (**4** *criticise*) _____ by employees ever since it (**5** *introduce*) _____ just over two years ago, notable improvements in productivity and quality (**6** *notice*) _____ . However, management is keen to take some of the criticism on board and has announced that the pay system (**7** *review*) _____ in two months. Therefore, employees (**8** *currently/encourage*) _____ to provide feedback on the system through informal channels of communication. Furthermore, a suggestions box (**9** *also/provide*) _____ for anyone who wishes to make a proposal anonymously. The suggestions box (**10** *can/find*) _____ next to the clocking-in machine by the staff notice board.

1 Put the following steps of the executive search process into the correct order.

❏ The client appoints one of the candidates.

❏ The headhunter identifies possible candidates.

❏ The candidates are interviewed by the headhunter.

❏ The client instructs the headhunter to fill a vacancy.

❏ The headhunter provides a shortlist of candidates.

❏ The client pays the headhunter his completion fee.

❏ Candidates go through the client's selection process.

2 Match the words as they appear in the unit.

1	recruitment	location
2	extension	agency
3	future	player
4	executive	shortage
5	neutral	reference
6	key	information
7	sensitive	search
8	skills	number

3 Complete each sentence with a suitable preposition.

1 Headhunting is _____ the increase as advertising becomes less and less cost-effective.

2 Headhunters are able to target people who are not actually _____ the job market.

3 A headhunter will always make a careful note of names _____ future reference.

4 Recruitment in the UK is divided _____ agency recruitment, advertising or executive search.

5 Headhunters can offer companies access _____ commercially sensitive information.

6 Executive search firms monitor Internet forums, noting any interesting names they come _____ .

7 The headhunter assists _____ the offer process.

8 You don't need to be fed up _____ your job to be susceptible to an approach from a headhunter.

9 A brilliant contribution _____ an Internet forum could possibly attract the attention of a headhunter.

4 Match the words.

1	fill	a list
2	present	a vacancy
3	shortlist	business
4	pay	findings
5	conduct	a retainer
6	compile	candidates

5 Use the words to write sentences with *recruit(ment)*.

Candidates go through our recruitment process.

apply   agency

qualities   candidates   process

sector   method

job   (recruit(ment))   skills

CV   performance   shortlist

appoint   vacancy

headhunter

6 Complete the table.

Verb	Noun
apply	....
....	appointment
compare	....
explain	....
....	category
recruit	....

Reference words

7 Complete the text by filling each gap with a suitable reference word.

There are several methods a company can use when looking to fill staff vacancies. Each of (1) _these_ methods has its own advantages and disadvantages. When deciding (2) _____ of these to use, the company must first consider (3) _____ objectives. For instance, 'advertising selection', (4) _____ is placing an advertisement in a newspaper or magazine, is most suitable for (5) _____ vacancies which do not require particularly high levels of specialised knowledge. At the other end of the scale is the expensive process of 'executive search', (6) _____ is also known as 'headhunting'. (7) _____ method involves the company contracting a specialist to identify candidates (8) _____ best match its needs. Companies can only justify going to (9) _____ expense when they feel it will be difficult to fill a position using traditional methods. Between (10) _____ two extremes is a further method: agency recruitment.

Exam practice

Reading Test Part One

- Look at the sentences below and the five news bulletins.
- Which bulletin does each sentence refer to?
- For each sentence **1 - 8**, mark **one** letter **A**, **B**, **C**, **D** or **E**.
- You will need to use some of the letters more than once.

Example

0   This company has suspended plans to work closely with another company.

A   B   C   D   E
■   ☐   ☐   ☐   ☐

---

1   This company will be working with a government organisation.
2   This company's decision to restructure will result in staff shortages.
3   This company is to reduce the number of administrative posts.
4   This company will sell off assets to offset poor financial results.
5   This company has made cuts which are unpopular with senior staff.
6   This company is in the process of upgrading some of its facilities.
7   This company has postponed its entry into new western European markets.
8   This company is suffering from the effects of increased competition.

A   **Taler to cut UK workforce**

Taler Chemicals, the Anglo-German industrial chemical company, announced yesterday that it is to cut 600 blue-collar jobs in a series of downsizing measures at three of its British plants. The news coincided with confirmation that the company also plans to dispose of its loss-making operations, CapPaints, the industrial solvent and paint division. This restructuring comes as the company reported a sharp drop in pre-tax profits. According to a company spokesman, the proposed joint venture with DTR International, one of Taler Chemicals' main competitors, is likely to be shelved.

B   **Merger creates Hungarian software powerhouse**

Silcom has finalised merger terms with ARER to create one of Hungary's largest computer software companies. Details of the merger are expected to be released later today. However, it is believed that Silcom's plans to break into France and Germany have been put on hold for the time being and that major job losses will soon be announced. Silcom looks set to benefit from the merger with ARER, which has recently been awarded a number of major contracts, including a contract with the Hungarian Ministry for Foreign Affairs, which will be worth in excess of $345,000 for the company.

C   **Profit warning at LYT International**

LYT International, one of Europe's leading Management Training Organisations, has warned shareholders to expect a fall in full year profits. The company, whose flagship training centre in Copenhagen is currently being modernised and refurbished, made an interim profit of $12m, compared with $23m in 1998. In response to its poor financial results, LYT has announced plans to cut jobs in its French and Spanish centres. An employee spokesman said that the move would prove unpopular and that with insufficient employees, some centres would struggle to deliver the high level of service demanded.

D | **Shake-up at BTED**
Nina Rantanen, former government adviser and the new CEO at BTED Power in Finland, has announced cost-cutting measures at the company. This decision has already led to the resignation of one of the company's most respected employees. Annika Ehlers had been with BTED Power for over 20 years, most recently as its Head of Operations. It is believed that she objected to company plans to reduce staffing levels at two of BTED Power's plants. Indications are that further high level resignations will follow in the next few months.

E | **Restructuring plans announced at San Freight**
San Freight has responded to redundancy rumours by revealing that it is to cut the number of office-based staff employed in its Scandinavian division by 25% over the next 24 months. The announcement follows confirmation that the company has also decided to postpone the planned upgrading of haulage systems at its Stockholm subsidiary. A senior staff member has revealed that San Freight's business has deteriorated in recent months due to the escalating price war with central and eastern European rivals.

Reading Test Part Five

- Read the article below about corporate hospitality.
- For each question **1 - 10**, write **one** word.

Example

0 | A | S | | | | | | |

Corporate hospitality

In recent years there has been a noticeable growth in the number of operators offering corporate hospitality services. One of the most successful is *Truffles!*, which organises tailor-made corporate events **(0)** ..... varied as conferences and trade-fairs.

What makes *Truffles!* special is the way in **(1)** ..... the company carefully researches clients' needs and offers tailor-made advice. *Truffles!* also offers a wide range of supplementary services to complement its main venue-finding service, **(2)** ..... the majority of its competitors, who concentrate on the venue-finding side of the business.

Truffles! promises to find companies exactly the right setting for their corporate event, **(3)** ..... unusual the request may be. Venues include not **(4)** ..... the familiar large city centre hotels but also more unusual locations, such as wine cellars. *Truffles!* claims that **(5)** ..... of the venues it represents is checked regularly, which means that guests can be assured of consistently high standards.

Some of the most popular choices are the residential centres situated in the heart of Britain's finest countryside. One rarely finds, for example, as superb **(6)** ..... venue as *Watercress House* at such competitive rates. This elegant country house can accommodate up to 45 delegates in en suite rooms which include **(7)** ..... special features as direct-dial telephones, well-lit desks and modem sockets.

The main conference suite is located on the second floor and enjoys outstanding views over the surrounding countryside. Two further conference rooms are available, **(8)** ..... of which can accommodate up to 20 delegates.

Watercress House is just **(9)** ..... of the many splendid country houses represented by *Truffles!*, who currently have no fewer **(10)** ..... 50 such exceptional venues on their books.

Corporate culture

What shapes corporate culture?

Speaking ❶ What can the following tell you about a company's culture?

- mission statement
- organisational hierarchy
- company buildings
- dress code

Reading ❷ IKEA, the Swedish furniture retailer, promotes a single corporate culture throughout its international operations. Read the extract opposite from an IKEA brochure and make notes under the following headings.

Company values Werte	shared: simple + optimistic lifestyle natural way of working together not exaggerated respect as complicated regulation
Company policies Richtlinien	no status symbols – care for employees as person people internal promotion – praise + rebuke question, renew, change – careful recruitment
Staff profile	– people to build upon / loyal – ... that promote the company culture – strong enough to question / put across – promote development

A strong and living corporate culture

IKEA has a strong and living corporate culture. It has grown step by step, bit by bit, along with our business idea. Our culture and business idea are the cornerstones of our operations. They support and strengthen each other. Our corporate culture helps us to retain the spirit and vitality of the early years, and to create a feeling of belonging in a large international organization. Our corporate culture is what binds us together.

Our corporate culture is based on shared values: a simple and optimistic lifestyle, a natural way of working and being together, without imposing exaggerated respect and complicated regulations. The key words are simplicity and humility, thrift, a sense of responsibility, enthusiasm and flexibility. Perhaps the most important of these is simplicity, as seen in the unpretentious way we associate with each other. There are no status symbols to create barriers between managers and their fellow workers. Our customers don't expect to pay for first-class hotels, directors' dining rooms and flashy cars.

It is important that all employees share our basic values. We take a lot of trouble with recruitment. IKEA is an ideas company. Our business idea and culture provide us with a framework, and we look for people to build upon and promote our culture. But we also want people who can cut across our organization, who are strong enough to question, renew and change. Such people promote development and should be encouraged not punished.

Internal promotion is still the norm, but we also recruit a number of people from outside. This is essential for strong expansion. And it provides us with new impulses.

Keeping our culture alive is management's key task. The best way is to set a good example and care about the employees. To see the person behind the professional. Caring means listening and encouraging new ideas and fresh initiatives, action and a sense of responsibility. Caring also means following up, putting right what goes wrong. Being able to praise and rebuke.

Our managers must know their job, and personally involve themselves in detail. "Retail is detail." Battles are seldom won at the desk. They are won out in the real world.

Simplicity and efficiency are usually synonymous concepts. Today we are a long way from our goals. We must put this right. At all levels. Then we will feel happier with each other and with our tasks. The continued success of IKEA rests on the involvement and enthusiasm of individual employees. And a great deal depends on our managers' perceptiveness and ability to care.

Language ❸ Look at the gerund and infinitive in the following sentences. Find further examples of these forms in the text and discuss how they are used.

Keeping our culture alive is management's key task.
Our corporate culture helps us to retain the spirit and vitality of the early years.

Speaking ❹ In what ways is your own company culture similar or different to IKEA's?

Småland in Sweden, where IKEA's founder Ingvar Kamprad grew up

The IKEA way

Listening 1 ❶ Göran Nilsson, Managing Director of IKEA UK, talks about the company's corporate culture. Listen and choose one letter for the correct answer.

Göran Nilsson
Managing Director
IKEA UK

1 How alike are all IKEA's stores worldwide?
   A Each store has the same management practices. ✓
   B Each store carries a different product range.
   C Each store is adapted to the local culture.

2 What was the main influence on the formation of IKEA's values?
   A traditional Swedish values ✓
   B Ingvar Kamprad's personal values
   C different cultural values within IKEA ✓

3 IKEA can cope with the diversity of its workforce because
   A its managers have international experience.
   B its basic corporate values are found in all cultures. ✓
   C its employees interpret IKEA beliefs differently.

4 What is the main advantage of a strong corporate culture?
   A It makes international transfers easier.
   B It reduces the cost of global marketing.
   C It stops competitors copying IKEA. ✓

5 What is IKEA's main policy for educating its staff?
   A It produces educational videos and brochures.
   B It holds special training sessions for managers. ✓
   C It encourages regular meetings to discuss culture. ✓

6 How does IKEA's culture affect its recruitment process?
   A Candidates are assessed on their personal qualities. ✓
   B Highly skilled candidates are attracted to vacancies.
   C Candidates from a retail background are preferred.

Nadine
2 + 5 + 8

7   What role does culture play in promotion decisions at IKEA?
    A   Only Swedes can become senior managers.
    B   A knowledge of Swedish culture is vital for promotion. ✓
    C   Nationality plays no part in promotion decisions.

8   Since the mid-1980s IKEA's development has been most affected by the
    A   stepping down of Ingvar Kamprad as President.
    B   challenge of increasingly competitive markets.
    C   way it has expanded over the last ten years. ✓

Speaking **②**   What does your company do to promote its corporate culture?

Listening 2 **③**   Five IKEA managers talk about IKEA and its founder, Ingvar Kamprad. Listen and decide
which core IKEA values each anecdote illustrates.

Speaker 1 ..... anti- bureaucratic

Speaker 2 ..... Informal / casual atmosphere   openness

Speaker 3 ..... Direct contact Mgt / Employee / friendly enthusiastic

Speaker 4 ..... Transparent planing   simplicity

Speaker 5 ..... Simplicity (low price)   humility

Speaking **④**   Think of an anecdote to illustrate one of your company's core values.

Writing **⑤**   Write a 200-250 word statement of your company's culture for the English version of a
promotional brochure. Include information on your company's values and practices.

Optional task **⑥**   Visit the www.ikea.com website and prepare a short presentation about IKEA's history
and global expansion.

Cultural diversity

How culture influences business

Speaking ❶ ·What factors affect decision-making in these areas in your country?

- recruiting new employees
- promoting staff
- fixing salary levels
- making staff redundant

Reading 1 ❷ Look at the article on the opposite page about a research project which examines the effect of cultural values on management decision-making. Choose the best sentence to fill each gap.

A This relationship is based on shared expectations which are common to employees of the same nationality.

B Typical of this is the belief that individuals should receive salary gains without having to share them with lower-performance colleagues.

C These take the form of one-page problem scenarios, each one centred on a specific issue.

D However, without this awareness, employees from diverse nationalities cannot appreciate their differences and build mutual understanding.

E Most international human resources managers will have experienced these expectation differences at first hand.

F These sensitive areas touch directly upon cultural norms and people's sense of well-being and order.

G Decisions taken with the welfare of more than the individual in mind are characteristic of this value system.

H There is also the more complicated question: what reasons do they give to explain their choices?

Speaking ❸ Are decisions affecting each of the four areas based on group or market logic in your culture?

National cultures, international business

National culture is a major barrier to making global businesses effective. Different nationalities have different expectations as to how employers and employees should behave. Michaël Segalla describes how national values are directly related to organisational decision-making.

In today's hyper-competitive global markets, any company that operates internationally is faced with the task of integrating many value systems into a framework that allows the organisation not only to survive but also to compete effectively. A European research group - the European Managerial Decision Making Project - was formed in 1994 to examine the effect of different national value systems on organisational policy. The project's research methodology is simple: given identical business problems, do managers in six different European countries choose similar solutions? 0 H In addition to the responses to these two questions, the study also includes both organisational and personal data.

The behaviours that intrigue the research team most are decisions concerning recruitment, promotion, remuneration and workforce reductions. The criteria used to select, promote, pay and make employees redundant are thought to reveal most about national values. 1 E Decisions about finance and marketing, on the other hand, are far less emotive and less likely to reveal underlying values.

The researchers believe a strong bond exists between people's sense of well-being and their situation at work, that is, the way they get on with a work group or employer. 2 A For multinationals, therefore, an understanding of cultural diversity within the organisation is a prerequisite of effective employee relationships.

The research is based on semi-structured interviews with managers from 74 European banks. The managers are presented with common dilemmas focusing on the four key areas: recruitment, promotion, remuneration and reductions in the workforce. 3 C The respondents are asked to solve these dilemmas and give their reasoning.

The responses are then plotted between two opposing logics. The first is called 'group logic'. 4 G Even decisions such as who to promote or make redundant can sometimes be discussed in terms of their group effects. The second logic is an economic rationale, which the researchers called 'market logic'. Here decisions are based on the economic realities arising from the marketplace as opposed to group considerations. 5 B A summary of the study's findings is shown in Figure 1 (on the next page).

According to research, few people really know their own cultural values. 6 D This means that organisations need to approach cross-cultural training seriously as it can be critical to the success of an international venture. Simply bringing in a 'cultural expert' to talk about different national values is not an option. Although these seminars can be entertaining, they ultimately fail because they do not require managers to examine their own values first.

Adapted from the Financial Times, 7 March 1998

Reading 2 ④ Read the conclusions below from the European Managerial Decision Making Project. Which country does each colour refer to?

England	France	Germany	Italy	Spain
blue	brown	purple	yellow	red

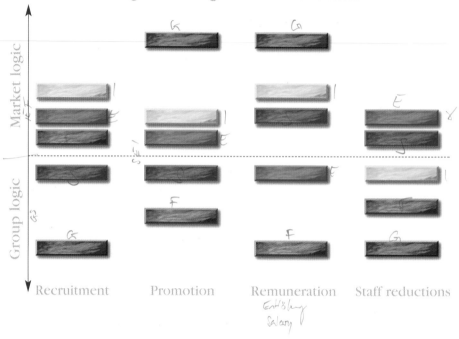

Figure 1: Management decision criteria

Market logic

Group logic

Recruitment   Promotion   Remuneration   Staff reductions
Entlohnung
Salary

The results of the survey are summarised below.

- In Italy, England and France respondents tended to use market logic in hiring new managers. They more often chose to hire foreign, multilingual employees with an elite general education. The German and Spanish managers followed the opposite strategy by hiring local managers with more technical training.

- The German sample stood nearly alone in its concern for promoting managers on the basis of objective performance criteria. In contrast, French managers based promotion on seniority or group loyalty criteria.

- The German sample stood alone again in its concern that remuneration should be based on measurable individual performance factors. Again the French sample held the extreme opposite belief that remuneration should be based on group, not individual performance.

- English managers most often based staff reduction decisions on the performance-to-salary ratio. More than 70 per cent of the English respondents would make redundant a middle-aged, high-salary manager with average performance. At the opposite end of the scale, less than 10 per cent of the German respondents would discharge the same manager. They would favour discharging young managers who could find jobs more easily, thereby preserving social stability.

Speaking ⑤ Choose two of the five countries. What difficulties might people from these countries experience when working together?

Building international teams

Work in groups. Your company is entering into an overseas joint venture. First decide on the details of the companies involved (nationalities, activities etc.). Then read the following e-mail and decide on a recruitment policy.

International Sales

From:	Jocelyn Garvie, Human Resources
Sent:	22 January 2000 09:59
To:	
Subject:	Recruitment policy for new joint venture

We need to discuss the management team for the new joint venture. We've decided we need a team of four but haven't thought about personal profiles yet. I've organised a meeting for next Tuesday and I suggest we think about the following issues.

- Ideal age, sex and nationality of the team members
- Recruitment policy (internal, national or international)
- Hierarchy and communication within the team
- Pay structure for the team members

Could you think about it and have some proposals ready for Tuesday? We'll be starting at 10 am. The meeting will be conducted in English as usual.

Agreeing and disagreeing

We often show agreement by repeating other people's words or completing their sentences. We can reinforce a proposal by adding supporting ideas.

- *I think that's the best way of doing it.*
- ▼ *I think that's the best way too. And it would save money.*

- *I think we should pay team bonuses.*
- ▼ *Which would encourage team spirit as well.*

In order to disagree effectively, it is important to give reasons or ask questions.

- *It would be a good idea to recruit internationally.*
- ▼ *That's true. But it would be more expensive.*

- *I think it's important to use Head Office staff.*
- ▼ *But who would you choose?*

Writing ❷   Write a 200-250 word letter to a business partner visiting your country. Give advice about attitudes to hierarchy, time, gender and anything else you think is important.

Optional task ❸   Choose a country and research the cultural attitudes which might affect the way you would do business there. Prepare a brief presentation on your findings.

1 Choose the correct word to fill each gap.

The number of training organisations in the country has been increasing at a rapid (1) _____ over the last decade and this trend seems set to continue. Management Worldwide Ltd is one of the country's most (2) _____ training organisations, with over 50 centres throughout the UK. Its focus is on a (3) _____ area: management skills training. Management Worldwide employs over a thousand people in areas as (4) _____ as accountancy, marketing, computing, sales and languages. It has a non-hierarchical approach to management and believes in giving (5) _____ to staff at all levels of the organisation. Its corporate (6) _____, as stated in the company's mission (7) _____ , include optimism, respect and flexibility. Management Worldwide's business goal is to increase shareholder value by concentrating on its (8) _____ training business and offering excellent service to clients.

1	A pace	B speed	C initiative
2	A successful	B exaggerated	C valuable
3	A reduced	B single	C uniform
4	A irregular	B flexible	C diverse
5	A initiative	B pressure	C responsibility
6	A strategies	B values	C qualities
7	A statement	B catalogue	C brochure
8	A core	B essential	C prime

2 Complete each sentence with the correct form of the word in capital letters.

1 ADAPT
We've only made minor product _____ for the North American market.

2 COMPETE
In the past, several of IKEA's _____ have tried to clone the company's store concept.

3 OPERATE
The company actively promotes a single company culture throughout its international _____ .

4 PROMOTE
The marketing division has produced a very flashy _____ brochure for the campaign.

5 INTERPRET
Some cultures may have different _____ of concepts like freedom and authority.

6 EXPAND
The rapid pace of _____ has had a big influence on the way the company has developed.

7 INFLUENCE
Our new CEO has been very _____ in reshaping our corporate culture.

8 PERCEIVE
I find her really _____ ; she notices what's going on, even when it's not obvious.

3 Match the words with a similar meaning.

1	diverse	new
2	similar	different
3	informal	hard
4	fresh	crucial
5	economical	worldwide
6	vital	thrifty
7	tough	casual
8	global	alike

Gerunds and infinitives

4 Complete the text. Put each verb in brackets into the correct form.

Birte Soltvedt has been the Managing Director of Denpak for five years now and it is easy (1 see) _to see_ the influence she has had in that time. Upon (2 arrive) _____ at Denpak, Soltvedt went about fundamentally modernising the Danish packaging company's way of (3 operate) _____ as well as (4 restructure) _____ its management. Although this came as a shock to many managers used to (5 work) _____ within a very strict hierarchy, the new, flatter management structure has helped Denpak (6 increase) _____ efficiency while (7 realise) _____ substantial cost savings at the same time. Considered by many (8 be) _____ a hard and uncompromising businesswoman, the 46-year-old Norwegian is happy enough (9 let) _____ people (10 believe) _____ this, even though she herself insists that in reality she really dislikes (11 confront) _____ people and worries about every decision she makes. Despite successfully managing (12 turn) _____ the company around, Soltvedt says there is no time (13 reflect) _____ on her achievements. Instead, she is busily planning the company's long-term growth strategy and implementing even more changes: 'It's essential that we keep (14 look) _____ to the future. The worst thing Denpak could possibly do now is stop (15 modernise) _____ just because the company happens (16 be) _____ back in profit.'

Complete the text with the following linking words and phrases.

while	therefore	however	similarly
means that	as opposed to	although	

Increased exposure to international business (**1**) _____ Japanese companies are not always as traditional as in the past. (**2**) _____ , there are still a number of important cultural factors which need to be considered when doing business in Japan.

- During negotiations, it is common for there to be long periods of silence (**3**) _____ your Japanese colleagues formulate their response.

- The Japanese will still usually avoid saying 'no'. You may (**4**) _____ leave a meeting with the wrong impression.

- Japanese meetings tend to be more formal than those in the USA, with people being addressed by their title and surname (**5**) _____ their first names.

- Dress is a very important issue for the Japanese, with a smart suit and tie the expected dress code in all business situations.

- Business remains still very much a male domain and (**6**) _____ inroads have been made by Japanese women, it is still unusual to find them in high level positions. (**7**) _____ , workers in senior positions tend to be older than their counterparts in the USA.

2 The graph shows the changing number of employees at two multinationals, 1996-2000. Write a 120-140 word report describing and comparing the two companies.

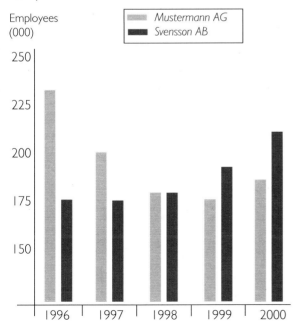

Employees (000)

Mustermann AG
Svensson AB

3 Match the words as they appear in the unit.

1	do	differences
2	fix	business
3	conduct	a strategy
4	appreciate	a belief
5	build	salary levels
6	solve	understanding
7	follow	a meeting
8	hold	a dilemma

4 Complete the table.

Verb	Noun
choose	....
....	success
expect	....
....	effect
pay	....
believe	....
....	solution
promote	....
....	diversity
examine	....
....	preservation

Modals

5 Use the exact form of the verb in brackets to rewrite the following sentences.

1 Perhaps the name of the product was the problem.
(*could*) The name of the product could have been the problem.

2 It was a waste of time going there.
(*needn't*)
_____

3 Adapting the product was a bad decision.
(*should*)
_____

4 It's time we were getting back.
(*ought*)
_____

5 Well, the language problems didn't help, did they?
(*can't*)
_____

6 Maybe they're having trouble working together.
(*might*)
_____

Reading Test Part Three

- Read the following article on business ethics and the questions on the opposite page.
- Each question has four suggested answers or ways of finishing the sentence, **A**, **B**, **C** and **D**.
- Mark **one** letter **A**, **B**, **C** or **D** for the answer you choose.

Companies turn to ethics for competitive advantage

In the old days measuring company performance was simply a case of looking at turnover, profits and dividends. However, the last few years have seen environmental and ethical issues move to the forefront of public concern and resulted in a closer scrutiny of a company's performance in terms of its business ethics. As the Government has been slow to respond to the increasing importance of ethics, companies have been forced to address the subject themselves and re-align their own management policies accordingly. These policies will determine how a company conducts all aspects of its business, from dealing with clients to reporting to shareholders.

By setting themselves up as ethical, however, companies are not so much promoting the importance of ethical conduct, the well-being of the local community or the development of society as a whole, as engaging in a powerful marketing and PR exercise to attract both discerning clients and bright young recruits. In today's markets, any company without a coherent ethics policy is in danger of surrendering a competitive advantage to its rivals.

In order to develop an ethical code of conduct, companies will have to deal with issues such as the legal implications of their disciplinary measures and the effect any new procedures will have on employees. However, new policies can only be developed once the company has identified the core values that underpin its day to day operations. Without a clear understanding of these values, it is impossible to develop a code of conduct compatible with the company's culture. An effective code will dictate how employees approach conflicts and other stressful dilemmas not covered by the normal terms and conditions of employment. It will provide employees with a clear understanding of what behaviour is expected when they find themselves confronted with such dilemmas.

Ethical procedures are particularly critical in times of crisis. Pay disputes, sexual harassment charges or cases of fraud, for example, can involve very complex issues that require careful decision-making and can have a very negative effect on staff morale. At such times it is crucial that companies act in an ethical manner. By doing so, they may not be able to avoid the potentially damaging publicity such cases inevitably attract; they will, however, be in a much stronger position to defend themselves in a court of law.

The major obstacle which companies face, having established a code of conduct, is that of ensuring that each individual member of staff follows it. Some organisations simply distribute leaflets to all staff in the hope that they will read and act on them. Other companies take a more active approach and invite management gurus to hold seminars on the subject, which, while often highly entertaining, have little long-term impact. Although some companies now include ethics as part of their standard induction programme, it is widely accepted that this is not enough. The issue of ethics in the workplace is now of such importance that it needs to be incorporated into in-company development programmes for all employees, from the shop floor to the boardroom.

With little sign of public concern abating, no organisation can afford to ignore the subject of ethics in the workplace. In order to address the issue effectively, companies need to ensure that staff at all levels feel committed to the company and its values and are motivated to transfer this commitment into ethical behaviour.

1   Business ethics are becoming more important as a result of

   A consumer demands.

   B shareholder concern.

   C management theories.

   D government legislation.

2   Why are companies promoting ethical practice?

   A to develop customer awareness of social issues

   B to help raise money for the local community

   C to enhance the positive image of the company

   D to improve the conduct of employees

3   What must companies do first to develop an ethical code?

   A take appropriate legal advice

   B consult employees at all levels

   C establish their basic principles

   D set up disciplinary procedures

4   A code of conduct helps employees

   A work together more effectively.

   B improve terms and conditions.

   C understand their duties better.

   D cope with difficult situations.

5   At times of crisis, a code of conduct reduces the

   A likelihood of negative publicity.

   B potential damage of legal action.

   C negative effect on staff morale.

   D time it takes to make decisions.

6   How can companies ensure that staff follow ethical procedures?

   A by distributing detailed leaflets to employees

   B by integrating ethics into training at all levels

   C by arranging seminars with ethics consultants

   D by including ethics in induction programmes

Writing Test Part Two (A)

- Your company is experiencing financial difficulties. Your manager has asked you to write a report considering ways of cutting costs in your department.
- Write a **report**, suggesting ways of cutting costs and explaining the implications these cuts might have on the running of your department.
- Write **200 - 250** words.

Reading Test Part Four

- Read the article below about cultural awareness in business.
- Choose the best word to fill each gap.
- For each question **1 - 10**, mark **one** letter **A**, **B**, **C** or **D**.
- There is an example at the beginning **(0)**.

Cultural awareness

To succeed in today's global market place, it is essential to learn as much as possible about the **(0)** ..... in overseas markets. In the past, companies with international aspirations simply familiarised themselves with any differences in the legal system or in the **(1)** ..... used in the day-to-day business of import and export.

Modern trade, however, **(2)** ..... more. Today the company seeking international success must also understand the people who live and work in countries they deal with, how they think, behave and do business. In short, today's market leaders must **(3)** ..... greater cultural awareness.

Business people operating in foreign markets often fail to consider that cultural differences can result in a **(4)** ..... of approaches to everyday business activities such as the way a cross-cultural team **(5)** ..... or how it conducts its meetings.

One of the main **(6)** ..... of investing in our cultural awareness programmes is that they can help you to fully **(7)** ..... your business potential, leaving you better placed to succeed. Our cultural awareness training seminars will **(8)** ..... the importance of taking into account how other nationalities think and behave and how they might see you. We can also help you develop the **(9)** ..... you need to construct effective working relationships and **(10)** ..... difficulties that may arise when working with colleagues or clients from different nationalities and cultures.

Example

0 A conditions   B elements   C influences   D factors

A   B   C   D
■□ □□ □□ □□

1	A technicalities	B mechanics	C schedules	D procedures
2	A commands	B requests	C demands	D prescribes
3	A procure	B find	C acquire	D earn
4	A variety	B scope	C choice	D selection
5	A co-operates	B associates	C contributes	D participates
6	A prizes	B benefits	C premiums	D compensations
7	A practise	B exploit	C outdo	D employ
8	A demonstrate	B expose	C announce	D publish
9	A talent	B skills	C strength	D proficiencies
10	A overturn	B overrun	C overtake	D overcome

Reading Test Part Five

- Read the article below about effective negotiating.
- For each question 1 - 10, write **one** word.

Example

```
0  A  L  S  O  □  □  □  □  □
```

Effective negotiating

We are always negotiating, not only in business, but **(0)** ..... in our private lives, from deciding what to watch on TV to deciding where to go on holiday. Rarely, in fact, **(1)** ..... any form of decision reached without some form of negotiation.

But **(2)** ..... we practise the art on a regular basis, it is always useful to review what we already subconsciously know. The following tips provide you **(3)** ..... strategies for negotiating effectively, no matter **(4)** ..... situation you find yourself in.

Firstly, try to make it a win-win situation. Start with the attitude that all parties should get something out of the deal. Look at the common ground, **(5)** ..... only at the gaps between you.

Secondly, try to find out what is cheap for you but valuable to your negotiating partner and vice versa. Exchanging something you don't want **(6)** ..... something you actually do want is, of course, the aim of **(7)** ..... parties involved.

Thirdly, be aware of your BATNA, your 'Best Alternative to a Negotiated Agreement'. You won't always get **(8)** ..... very deal you wanted so you need to bear in mind your best alternative if the negotiation fails. In fact, telling your negotiating partner, 'Thanks but I can get a better deal elsewhere' often brings about movement in the other side's position!

And finally, be creative. Think of the exercise **(9)** ..... both sides coming together to solve a common problem. Developing the valuable skills you need to negotiate most effectively takes time and effort, but by taking on just a **(10)** ..... simple techniques, you can make all the difference.

Writing Test Part Two (B)

- A trainee from one of your company's overseas subsidiaries is coming to work as your assistant for six months. Your boss has asked you to brief her on your company before she arrives.
- Write a **letter** to the trainee, describing the organisation of your company, the people she needs to know and the kind of work she will be doing. Include any further useful information which you think the trainee should know about your company.
- Write **200 - 250** words.

Industrial espionage

Research or espionage?

Speaking **1** How can a company access information about competitors? Which methods do you think are ethically acceptable?

Reading **2** Read the jumbled magazine article on the opposite page. What methods are mentioned in the article?

3 Now put the paragraphs into the correct order.

1 .A.
2 .....
3 .....
4 .....
5 .....
6 .....
7 .....

How secure is your business?

*All those spies who came in from the cold had to find somewhere to go, writes
Andrew Eames. So, like everyone else, they've gone into business.*

They may well be no more than urban legends but there's nothing quite like a good spy
story. Take for instance the tale of the Japanese executive who, while on a visit to a well-
known brewery, leaned over a vat and dangled the end of his tie into it. Back home, his tie was
analysed and his company was able to produce an imitation product.

B   What the court ruling shows is that without clear guidelines one man's espionage may be another
man's market research strategy. There is little evidence to show that bugging and infiltration are
on the increase but the fear of them certainly is. 'We are rapidly becoming far too paranoid in
relation to the size of the problem,' suggests business academic Stuart Macdonald. 'Companies
are confusing information exchange with industrial espionage. Information exchange is healthy;
no company can develop very far in isolation.'

C   However, despite increased spending on security, most people in the industry agree that the real
threat comes from within. Even hacking is not the problem it is reported to be. Far more common
is simply copying information onto disk and taking it home. A careless or disgruntled employee can
do far more damage than a bug in the coffee machine. 'In most cases when a company gets beaten
to a tender and suspects foul play, it'll be someone inside that's leaked crucial details,' says Ted
Clements of security consultants Pinkerton.

D   Well-managed and successful companies, according to Macdonald, have no need to resort to shady
practices. Such companies also tend to have motivated workers and therefore needn't worry
about the threat from within.

E   The problem is industrial spies steal information, not information containers, and information
carries no fingerprints. So how can a company protect itself from an employee who bears a grudge?
There are several simple precautions. Devise a system to control who has access to what level of
information; install passwords on computers; shred all paperwork and check personal details on
CVs. If you still have reason to suspect espionage, then look for warning signs in staff behaviour
and monitor the photocopier for any signs of late-night use.

F   Regardless of how much truth there is behind such stories, large companies take the threat of
industrial espionage very seriously. Eighty per cent of the Fortune 1,000 companies now maintain
in-house information security advisors. But does that mean there's lots of spying? In the absence
of anyone owning up, the only measure of activity is the turnover of the surveillance equipment
industry. Last year sales reached new records and were - say retailers - mostly made to businesses.

G   Solving the problem though is not a question of identifying the perpetrator and calling the police.
'It is no crime to commit industrial espionage,' pointed out the judge in a recent UK case, where
one car park company had infiltrated another. Only once the law is broken can the police take
action. By then, it's too late anyway.

*Adapted from **Business Life**, February 1997*

Speaking ④ Which measures mentioned in the article does your company take to protect itself from industrial espionage? What other measures does it take?

Information security

Listening 1 ❶ Rick Haywood, Managing Director of electronics wholesaler Octacon, discusses information security with two colleagues. Listen and identify the problem.

Listening 2 ❷ Listen to the rest of the discussion and complete the table.

Action discussed	Implications

3 Look at the conditional forms in the following sentences. Find further examples of these forms in the tapescripts and discuss how they are used.

*If there genuinely **is** a problem, then we**'ll have** to find out ...*
*If I **knew** that, we **wouldn't be** here.*

4 Complete the following information with phrases from the tapescripts.

Asking for clarification

The following phrases are useful when asking for clarification.

Are you saying ... ?

_____

_____

_____

_____

5 Your company wants to create a more open attitude towards internal information. Discuss and decide the following.

● what information should be available to staff
● the implications of the new policy

Your teacher will give you some cards with instructions.

Business ethics

What are business ethics?

Speaking ❶ Which of the following statements about ethics do you agree with?

- Ethics provide the rules within which an organisation must conduct itself.
- Ethics show an organisation's attitude towards society.
- Ethics are a source of competitive advantage.

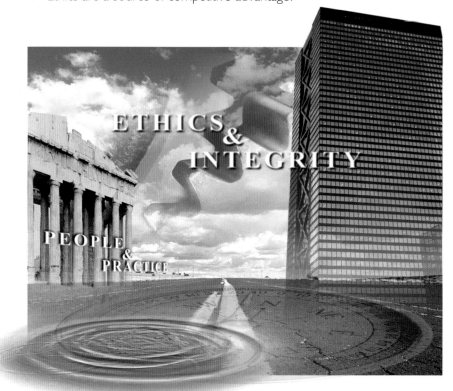

Reading ❷ Read the extract on the opposite page from the 1999 KPMG Business Ethics Survey. What did the CEOs consider the three most important features of an ethical organisation?

❸ Read the extract again. Are the following statements true or false?

1 The questionnaire was sent to a total of 1,000 senior executives.
2 It was thought to be of great importance to support good causes.
3 Fewer than half of the participating companies protect whistle-blowers.
4 Most CEOs were content with existing information security measures.

Language ❹ Look at the report again and find examples of the following.

1999 KPMG Business Ethics Survey:
Managing for Ethical Practice

Executive Briefing

Toronto, Canada
March 1999

In December 1998, KPMG sent a questionnaire to the CEOs of 1,000 Canadian companies, selected on the basis of size in terms of number of employees. In response to an increasing level of interest expressed by managers in the public sector, we extended our sample to include the senior executives of a further 225 organizations in the public sector.

The following points summarize our key findings.

■ When executives responding to our survey described an organization as 'highly ethical', the behaviours they gave the most weight to were legal compliance, fair employment practices and delivery of high-quality goods and services. Corporate philanthropy was given the least weight in making this judgement.

■ Written statements of values and principles were reported by 85% of participating organizations. The proportion of organizations with formal policies to protect employees who report ethical or legal violations (whistle-blowers) was 38%, an increase on the 22% reported in our 1997 survey.

■ The survey listed various issues and asked participants to indicate the level of management attention each received in their organization (shown below). Of these issues, the two most frequently identified as of greatest concern for the next three to five years were security of information and environmental issues. Security of information was also the issue with which respondents were least satisfied with current efforts.

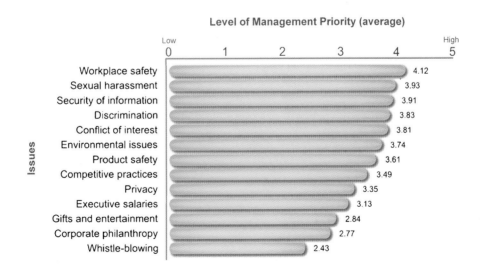

Level of Management Priority (average)

Issues	Priority
Workplace safety	4.12
Sexual harassment	3.93
Security of information	3.91
Discrimination	3.83
Conflict of interest	3.81
Environmental issues	3.74
Product safety	3.61
Competitive practices	3.49
Privacy	3.35
Executive salaries	3.13
Gifts and entertainment	2.84
Corporate philanthropy	2.77
Whistle-blowing	2.43

Speaking **5** Which ethical issues are you most concerned about in your company?

Listening ❶ Five people talk about unethical behaviour at their companies. Listen and decide which ethical issue and which consequence each speaker refers to.

Task one: ethical issue
Which ethical issue does each speaker refer to?

1 .....

2 .....

3 .....

4 .....

5 .....

A	industrial espionage
B	workplace safety
C	racial discrimination
D	environmental protection
E	executive salaries
F	sexual harassment
G	financial mismanagement
H	corporate gift-giving

Task two: consequence
Which consequence does each speaker refer to?

6 .....

7 .....

8 .....

9 .....

10 .....

I	a manager was dismissed
J	computer security was reviewed
K	an ethics officer was appointed
L	the company informed the police
M	a written warning was given
N	the company produced guidelines
O	a consultant was brought in
P	the employee resigned

Speaking ❷ Now put the five cases of unethical behaviour into order of seriousness.

Language **3** Look at the conditional forms in the following sentences. Find further examples of these forms in the tapescript and discuss how they are used.

If she'd complained to him in person, he'd have stopped doing it.
She warned them that she'd take legal action if nothing was done about it.

Speaking **4** Talk about one of the following topics for one minute.

- how to encourage ethical behaviour from employees
- the importance of ethics in today's business world

MORE MONEY FLOWS INTO ETHICAL INVESTMENT FUNDS

Neil James *is optimistic about the current trend of investment in the UK*

Companies face increased pressure on ethical reporting

Sarah Arnold reports on the Department of Trade and Industry's latest guidelines

JOB FITNESS TEST RULED AS DISCRIMINATION

...rimination in the work place. **Lucy Burgess**

Banks accused of discrimination against ethnic minorities

In a major new survey on discrimination...

HOME NEWS   10

Over 50s still face widespread discrimination

Michael Price watches with concern as t... port expo...

5

More companies now accept the concept of business ethics

...**emary Westgate** reports on the ...

Optional task **5** Visit the KPMG website, www.kpmg.com. Write a 200-250 word report evaluating the site, recommending improvements and giving reasons for your opinions.

1 Are the following examples of industrial espionage or measures against it?

1 infiltrate a competitor
2 monitor photocopier use
3 bug an office
4 hack into a network
5 shred important documents
6 leak sensitive information
7 bring in a security adviser
8 steal confidential data
9 identify a perpetrator
10 resort to shady practices
11 protect a computer system
12 install passwords

2 Some of the following lines contain an unnecessary word. Underline any extra words in lines 1-12.

1 Octacon, the electronics wholesaler, is worried about this
2 information security within the company. It has recently
3 lost several of major contracts to Centronics, its largest
4 competitor. Centronics seems to have been acquired
5 information regarding to the terms and conditions of
6 Octacon's existing contracts. It has targeted customers
7 each time their contracts were up for renewal. Octacon
8 suspects that a disgruntled employee who has been
9 leaking crucial details to their competitor or that
10 Centronics has managed to infiltrate by Octacon, for
11 example by hacking it into their corporate intranet. This
12 would be illegal, of course, but without a proof there is
little Octacon can do.

3 Complete the table.

Verb	Noun	Adjective
....	....	acceptable
suspect	....	....
....	imitation	....
access	....	....
analyse	....	....
....	security	....
protect	....	....
....	copy	....
identify	....	....
confuse	....	....
isolate	....	....
....	....	broken
measure	....	....

4 Match the words as they appear in the unit.

1 solve — paperwork
2 call — a problem
3 bear measures
4 devise a grudge
5 break foul play
6 suspect the police
7 shred the law
8 take a system

Conditionals

5 Complete the conversation. Put each verb in brackets into the correct form.

● Jill, it's Rick. I'm just calling to see whether you've come across anything in those appraisal files.

▼ Well, there are one or two interesting things but nothing shocking. If you (**1** *have*) _____have_____ a moment, I (**2** *come by*) _can come by_ and show you what I've found so far.

● Well, I'm just about to go into a meeting right now. But if you (**3** *be*) _____ free this afternoon, we (**4** *go*) _____ through it then. Why don't you give Oliver a call and see if he (**5** *be*) _____ around, as well?

▼ He's not in today. He's having a day off.

● That's a shame because it (**6** *be*) _____ good if we (**7** *also/look*) _____ at what he's found on the e-mail server.

▼ I (**8** *give*) _____ him a call at home if you (**9** *like*) _____ . He might be in.

● Good idea. Maybe he's got some print-outs or something in his desk which you could bring along.

▼ OK. But if he (**10** *not/have*) _____ anything, (**11** *you/still want*) _____ us to meet this afternoon?

● Yes. I mean, if he (**12** *not/find*) _____ anything worth mentioning last week, then he (**13** *not/need*) _____ come along to the meeting anyway.

▼ That's true. What if he (**14** *have*) _____ got something, though?

● Well, is he back tomorrow?

▼ I think so, yes.

● OK, call him first. If he (**15** *find*) _____ something, then we (**16** *put*) _____ the meeting off until tomorrow.

▼ OK. I'll get back to you when I've spoken to him.

1 Read through the unit and add more ethical issues.

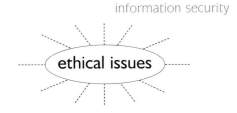

information security

ethical issues

Which issues do the following refer to?

1 employees copying confidential data onto disks

   information security

2 physically intimidating the opposite sex

   _____

3 accidents occurring at work

   _____

4 conforming to government legislation

   _____

5 senior managers receiving massive pay increases

   _____

6 rewarding clients with expensive freebies

   _____

7 not treating people from ethnic minorities equally

   _____

8 reporting breaches of a company's ethical code

   _____

2 Add a prefix to form the opposite of the following.

1 legal   ....
2 ethical   ....
3 fair   ....
4 lawful   ....
5 correct   ....
6 official   ....

3 Match the words with a similar meaning.

1 survey   precaution
2 measure   questionnaire
3 conduct   gift
4 rule   competitor
5 threat   regulation
6 rival   behaviour
7 freebie   warning

4 Fill each gap with a suitable word.

As you know, our company had been doing business out there for years, working with the smaller family-run firms. Nigel Beynon, (**1**) _____ was the Head of Purchasing for over fifteen years, had managed (**2**) _____ build up several solid relationships with local suppliers. In fact, I sometimes thought he felt (**3**) _____ at home out there than he (**4**) _____ back here in the UK. Anyway, problems first arose (**5**) _____ one of the newspapers decided to do a feature (**6**) _____ ethics in the clothing industry. They discovered (**7**) _____ one of our suppliers was using child labour. It was (**8**) _____ much of a shock to Nigel as it was to everyone (**9**) _____ . You see, he'd never actually visited (**10**) _____ single factory. He'd just believed the suppliers (**11**) _____ they assured him they conformed to our workplace standards. If only he (**12**) _____ taken the time to check their claims, he'd never have had to hand in his notice.

Conditionals

5 Complete the sentences. Put each verb in brackets into the correct form.

1 If she (*realise*) ___'d realised___ the report was confidential, she (*not/tell*) __wouldn't have told__ her friend about it.

2 The boss (*sack*) _____ him by now if he (*not/be*) _____ the Managing Director's nephew.

3 If we (*not/get*) _____ that contract, the company (*not/survive*) _____ the recession last year.

4 I'm sure she (*dismiss*) _____ if anyone (*find out*) _____ how she was getting her information.

5 If she (*not/film*) _____ shredding the files, she (*still/work*) _____ here today.

6 The problem (*solve*) _____ more quickly if the company (*bring*) _____ in a consultant earlier.

7 The company (*not/know*) _____ if the new assistant (*not/blow*) _____ the whistle to the press.

8 If he (*leave*) _____ sooner than he did, the company (*not/have*) _____ all the bad publicity it is right now.

Reading Test Part Two

- Read the health and safety guidelines.
- Choose the best sentence from **A - H** to fill in each of the gaps.
- For each gap **I - 6**, mark **one** letter **A - H**.
- Do not mark any letter more than once.
- There is an example at the beginning **(0)**.

Health and Safety Guidelines - Visual Display Units (VDUs)

In order to eliminate risk to the health and safety of employees, appliances should be used in accordance with suppliers' and manufacturers' instructions. As far as is reasonably practicable, all appliances should be kept in a good state of repair. **0** H Any appliance which is consequently found to be faulty or potentially dangerous should, where possible, be immediately isolated from the electrical supply and reported to a supervisor.

It is required by law that employees using VDUs should have regular breaks. **1** In both cases supervisors are responsible for ensuring that these breaks are observed. The company provides word processors which have been specially selected to provide a safe system of work and every effort has been made to ensure that they have been ergonomically designed. **2** This may be due to individual physical characteristics of the operator rather than the machine itself. In such cases, the company is obliged to take every action to improve the situation.

All employees are expected to notify their manager about any discomfort experienced whilst using a word processor. **3** Where entries refer to eyesight, display screen users are entitled, upon request, to a free eye test, the cost to be met by the company. If a user is said by his/her optician to require frequent eye tests, the employer should meet the costs of all necessary tests. **4** Operators are otherwise entitled to one free eye test every twelve months unless there are exceptional medical circumstances which have arisen during the period between examinations.

The development of office networks has resulted in modular configurations, comprising a number of interchangeable computers which may be easily moved around. **5** Moreover, employees should take care to ensure that no undue strain is caused through lifting in the wrong way.

It is the responsibility of all employees to report accidents. **6** This may help prevent a more serious incident from happening in the future.

A Any such complaints should be recorded in the company's Health and Safety log book.

B A supervisor should be notified immediately of all occurrences, however minor, so that appropriate action can be taken.

C These should be taken regardless of whether they follow a period of intense or occasional use.

D Attention is drawn to the possible dangers in seeking to carry too heavy a load.

E However, in some cases, the operation of such equipment can have an adverse effect.

F Hazards such as these must be reported immediately to the manager or any other person authorised to act on his or her behalf.

G This provision is restricted to situations where the need arises because of the employee's work.

H For this reason, visual display equipment should be regularly checked for damage.

Reading Test Part Six

● In **most** lines of the following text, there is **one** unnecessary word. It is either grammatically incorrect or does not fit in with the sense of the text.

● For each numbered line **1 - 12**, find the unnecessary word. Some lines are correct. If a line is correct, write **CORRECT**.

● The exercise begins with two examples **(0)** and **(00)**.

Example

0 | C | O | R | R | E | C | T | | |

00 | L | O | N | G | | | | | |

Working overseas

0 We are currently recruiting engineers, nurses, teachers and managers for

00 placements of six months long in a variety of locations worldwide.

1 Working overseas can offer you a once in a lifetime opportunity to live,

2 work and build the friendships in a very different environment. This

3 experience which will also give you a chance to widen your outlook on life,

4 encounter with cultural differences and develop new skills. To join us, you

5 must be fully qualified and have at least two years' full-time experience. In

6 addition to being resourceful, and you must be able to show sensitivity to

7 cultural differences. Flexibility that is also an extremely important quality;

8 you should be able to imagine what yourself happily adapting to new

9 standards of behaviour and dress, different food and even opening hours.

10 We will provide you a comprehensive package which includes free travel,

11 subsidised accommodation and a generous local salary. If you would like to

12 receive a further information on working for us overseas, please do not

hesitate to contact us on 020 8675 8982.

Writing Test Part Two

● Your company has received a number of complaints from staff about their working conditions. The Human Resources Manager has asked you to write a report about the current situation.

● Write the **report**, including the reasons for the complaints and recommendations for dealing with them.

● Write **200 - 250** words.

Global brands

Making brands global

Speaking **1** What foreign brands do you buy? Why?

2 Complete the table below with the following brands and industries.

Coca-Cola   Automobiles
Disney   Diversified
IBM   Semiconductors
Marlboro   Software
McDonald's   Telecoms

World's top 10 brands by value, June 1999

	Brand name	Origin	Industry	Value ($m)
1	*CC*	USA	Beverages	83,845
2	Microsoft	USA	*Software*	56,654
3	*IBM*	USA	Computers	43,781
4	General Electric	USA	*Diversified*	33,502
5	Ford	USA	*Automobiles*	33,197
6	*Disney*	USA	Entertainment	32,275
7	Intel	USA	*Semiconductors*	30,021
8	*McD.*	USA	Food	26,231
9	AT&T	USA	*Telecoms*	24,181
10	*Marlboro*	USA	Tobacco	21,048

Reading **3** Look at the three aspects of a brand as illustrated below. Which aspects of the following brands do you think are global?

Coca-Cola   Mars   Hertz   Nike   Barilla   Nescafé

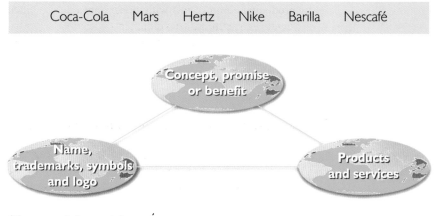

Concept, promise
or benefit

Name,
trademarks, symbols
and logo

Products
and services

Now read the article and compare your answers.

What are global brands and do they make sense? Jean-Noël Kapferer reports on the advantages of the global brand.

N o-one disagrees with the economic necessity of geographically extending a product. Not only does it increase turnover but it also makes economies of scale possible, thus giving companies a competitive advantage in local markets. But how far do we push the global idea? Should we globalise all aspects of a brand: its name, its creative concept and the product itself?

Global branding implies the wish to extend all three aspects throughout the world. Rarely, though, is it realistic and profitable to extend all of them. The Mars brand, for example, is not absolutely global. The Mars chocolate bar is sold as an all-round nutritious snack in the UK and as an energiser in Europe (different concepts and positioning for the same physical product). Nestlé adapts the taste of its worldwide brands to local markets. The Nescafé formulas vary worldwide.

Nowhere is globalisation more desirable than in sectors that revolve around mobility, such as the car rental and airline industries. When a brand in these sectors is seen as being international, its authority and expertise are automatically accepted. Companies such as Hertz, Avis and Europcar globalised their advertising campaigns by portraying typical images such as the busy executive. An Italian businessman will identify more with a hurried businessman who is not Italian than with an Italian who is not a businessman.

The main aim of such global marketing campaigns is not to increase sales but to maximise profitability. For example, instead of bringing out different TV advertisements for each country, a firm can use a single film for one region. The McCann-Erikson agency is proud of the fact that it has saved Coca-Cola $90m over the past 20 years by producing commercials with global appeal.

Social and cultural developments provide a favourable platform for globalisation. When young people no longer identify with long-established local values, they seek new models on which to build their identity. They are then open to influence from abroad. When drinking Coca-Cola, we all drink the American myth - fresh, young, dynamic, powerful, all-American images. Nike tells young people everywhere to surpass themselves, to transcend the confines of their race and culture.

Globalisation is also made easier when a brand is built around a cultural stereotype. AEG, Bosch, Siemens, Mercedes and BMW rest secure on the 'Made in Germany' model, which opens up the global market since the stereotype goes beyond national boundaries. People everywhere associate the stereotype with robust performance.

Barilla is another example: it is built on the classic Italian image of tomato sauce, pasta, a carefree way of life, songs and sun. IKEA furniture epitomises Sweden. Lancôme expresses the sophistication of the French woman.

Certain organisational factors ease the shift to a global brand. American firms, for instance, are naturally geared towards globalisation because marketing in their huge domestic market already treats America as a single entity despite its social and cultural differences.

Another organisational factor concerns the way US companies first expanded in Europe. Many set up European headquarters, usually based in Brussels or London. From early on Europe was considered a single and homogeneous area.

Finally, a single centre of production is also a great advantage. Procter & Gamble centralises European production of detergents in its Amiens factory. This maximises product standardisation and enables innovations to spread to all countries at once, thus giving the company a competitive advantage over local rivals and ensuring the continued growth and success of the brand.

*Adapted from the **Financial Times**, 30 January 1998*

4 Read the article again and choose one letter for the correct answer.

  I   To globalise a brand successfully, it is essential to
      A   globalise the product, its name, logo and concept.
      B   choose which parts of the brand need globalising.
      C   adapt the product to local market requirements.
      D   select a brand connected with international travel.

2 Companies such as Hertz globalise their advertisements by using
   A national character types.
   B successful executives.
   C Italian businessmen.
   D universal stereotypes. ✓

3 What is the main aim of global marketing campaigns?
   A to improve margins
   B to maximise turnover
   C to cut advertising costs
   D to increase product appeal

4 Young people are a good target for globalised products because they
   A have a great deal of spending power.
   B distance themselves from traditional ideas. ✓
   C are easily influenced by advertising.
   D want to live an Americanised lifestyle.

5 Cultural stereotypes can help globalise a product when the
   A customers like the nationality of the stereotype.
   B culture is known for high production standards.
   C associations match the type of product. ✓
   D target market is a cosmopolitan culture.

6 Why have American companies been so successful at globalisation?
   A They are good at adapting products to local tastes.
   B They choose good locations for European headquarters.
   C They are accustomed to selling to a large diverse market. ✓
   D They always centralise production at a single factory.

Language ❺ **Look at the word order in the following sentence. What do you notice about it? Find further examples of this pattern in the article and discuss how it is used.**

*Not only **does** it **increase** turnover but it also makes economies of scale possible.*

Speaking ❻ **Think of an internationally-known brand from your country which makes use of cultural stereotypes. What are the values associated with the stereotypes?**

Promoting a brand

Speaking **1** Have you bought any of these companies' products? Why/why not?

2 Choose one of the companies. How does it promote its brands in your country? Discuss the following.

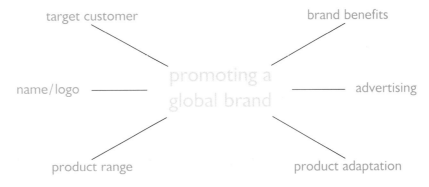

target customer

brand benefits

name/logo ——— promoting a global brand ——— advertising

product range

product adaptation

Now give a brief summary of your ideas.

3 Talk about one of the following topics for one minute.

- the importance of a global presence
- how to promote an imported brand
- the importance of stereotypes in advertising

Writing **4** Think of a successful domestic brand in your country. Write a 200-250 word proposal on how the brand could be globalised.

Optional task **5** Visit the L'Oréal website at www.loreal.com. Prepare a short presentation on the company's brands and markets.

Global sourcing

Choosing a supplier

Speaking ❶ What types of supplier does your company use? What criteria does your company apply when choosing suppliers?

❷ Companies tend to consider four main criteria when choosing a supplier. Complete the table below with the following measurements.

Per cent defective	$ per unit
Satisfaction surveys	Number of new product launches a year
Time to market	Total number of days late
Warranty dollars spent	Number of items in the catalogue

Main criteria when choosing a supplier		
Criteria	**Definitions**	**Measurements**
Cost	Cost relative to our competitors	
Quality	Conformance to standards Performance Reliability	Per cent defective
Delivery	Speed Reliability	
Flexibility	Product range New product introduction	

3 Think of a supplier to your company. What are its strengths and weaknesses?

Supplier relationships

Craig Barksdale, consultant Jefferson Watson

Listening **1** Craig Barksdale, a consultant at Jefferson Watson, talks about different types of supplier relationship. Listen and choose one letter for the correct answer.

1 Global sourcing has become so widespread because of the increasing
   A number of international mergers.
   B competitiveness of foreign markets.
   C efficiency of global communications.

2 What is the main attraction of global sourcing?
   A access to overseas markets
   B increased profit margins
   C quicker delivery times

3 What is the most common mistake companies make when sourcing globally?
   A They fail to consider all their important objectives.
   B They ignore the effect it might have on their image.
   C They forget to allow for exchange rate fluctuations.

4 When deciding on criteria for choosing a supplier, managers should
   A insist on consistently outstanding performance.
   B list and prioritise all their main objectives.
   C be as flexible as possible with their criteria.

5 What is the most important decision once a partner is selected?
   A how long-term the relationship should be
   B how the arrangement should be structured
   C how any information should be shared

6 What is the main advantage of 'buying the market'?
   A Little interaction is needed with suppliers.
   B Bidding process times are a lot quicker.
   C Administration costs are greatly reduced.

7 Strategic alliances make sense when
   A components are mutually dependent.
   B projects have a high level of financial risk.
   C development programmes are long-term.

8 Ownership of the supplier is preferable when
   A a company relies heavily on overseas suppliers.
   B cost savings are the most important factor.
   C access to vital resources is variable.

Speaking **2** What would be the most suitable type of supplier relationship in the following situations? Would it make sense for these companies to source globally?

   ● a car manufacturer sourcing a brake system
   ● a toy company sourcing a range of plastic dolls
   ● a restaurant sourcing its food supplies

Global sourcing

Reading **❶** QuayWest, a European clothing company, has shortlisted five suppliers for its new range of leisurewear. Match each of the following statements with a company below. Then give each supplier a rating (from 1 to 5) for price, quality, delivery and flexibility.

1 This supplier is able to offer a wide range of products.
2 There is a lot of old machinery in this supplier's factory.
3 This supplier is able to manufacture to the highest standards.
4 Orders are delivered extremely quickly by this supplier.
5 This supplier is hoping to improve its delivery times in the near future.
6 Doing business with this supplier could harm the company's reputation.
7 This supplier would be unable to adapt its product lines quickly.
8 This is the best supplier in terms of the relationship between price and quality.

Consort Trading Co. Ltd.
Yungtong-Dong 968, Korea **CTC**

Price .... Quality .... Delivery .... Flexibility ....

By far the most reasonably priced of the potential suppliers, this medium-sized company exports to many countries in Asia, the Pacific Rim and Europe. The company is well-established and employs a large but poorly paid workforce. This, along with obvious lack of investment in new plant, probably explains how the company is able to produce at such exceptionally low costs. These factors, however, also account for the modest quality of the goods, some of which could even fail to meet European standards. It seems that the supplier would be in a position to deliver within satisfactory times and the owners insist that they would be flexible enough to deal with last-minute orders. However, a supplier relationship with this company could possibly have serious PR implications.

S *Samokovska, Inc.*
Plodiv 4003, Bulgaria

Price .... Quality .... Delivery .... Flexibility ....

This small but very modern company has been supplying EU countries for several years now. This experience shows in the level of workmanship and has resulted in the company adopting a policy of ensuring that each item within its catalogue conforms to all EU specifications. However, the variety of the catalogue is somewhat limited - as is the company's production capacity. It appears the company has decided on a strategy of offering an exclusive selection of high-quality, expensive products. It seems unlikely that the company would be versatile enough to respond quickly enough to market changes or deal with orders at short notice. Moreover, although the delivery times are quite impressive, the company would struggle to maintain these when faced with larger orders.

The Namlong Sportswear Company Ltd.
Bangkok 10150, Thailand Namlong

Price .... Quality .... Delivery .... Flexibility ....

One of the largest textile suppliers in Thailand, the Namlong Sportswear Company is a large enterprise with several factories in the Bangkok area. The company employs a large workforce and relies extensively on manual labour. However, the scale of its resources means it is very flexible and its production cycles are relatively short, even for large orders. These factors, along with impressive distribution, allow the company to respond to any changes in order specifications or schedules while meeting tight deadlines. There may be some room for negotiation on prices, which look relatively expensive compared to many of Namlong's competitors in the area, especially when the slightly disappointing standard of workmanship is taken into account.

Shiva *Shiva Trading Co. Ltd.*
Mumbai 400034, India

Price .... Quality .... Delivery .... Flexibility ....

The Shiva Trading Company is a small but well-established family-owned business that has been exporting throughout the sub-continent and is now looking to enter the European market. To help with this expansion, it is offering very reasonable prices to potential European customers, especially in relation to the satisfactory levels of quality that its products display. On the other hand, its present size and limited capacity could lead to delays and a certain amount of inflexibility in terms of schedules and short notice orders. However, the owners insist that planned expansion of the premises will ease these pressures by increasing capacity and reducing production cycles, thus enabling the company to turn orders around more efficiently.

Hai Xin Group Co. Ltd.
Shanghai 200051, China **HAI XIN**

Price .... Quality .... Delivery .... Flexibility ....

This dynamic young company is looking for sales outlets in Europe. Although its goods tend to be slightly pricey, their quality is acceptable, with some evidence of attention to detail. However, it is not clear as yet whether these goods will conform to all EU regulations. The owners are confident, though, that their modern machinery and flexible production processes mean that the company will be able to cope with any changes in product specifications and garment features necessary to meet legal requirements. This flexibility also means that the company has already built up an impressively varied catalogue, with many items offering optional and additional features. This would suggest that introducing new product lines would not be a problem. Hai Xin also appears able to offer satisfactory delivery times.

Speaking ❷ You work in the QuayWest Purchasing Department. Discuss and decide the following.

- your key criteria for suppliers of the new range of leisurewear
- which of the five suppliers would be the most suitable

Writing ❸ Write a 200-250 word report recommending the most suitable supplier for QuayWest and giving reasons for your decision.

QUALITY
LEISUREWEAR
AFFORDABLE
PRICES

QUAYWEST
CALL 0800 599478 FOR DETAILS OF YOUR NEAREST STOCKIST.

1 Complete the sentences with the correct form of the following words.

universe	adaptation	profit	advertisement
globe	culture	diversity	product

1 Coca-Cola's marketing campaigns always transcend _____ differences.

2 Companies no longer have to develop different _____ campaigns for different countries.

3 To begin with, a company has to decide whether or not to _____ all aspects of the brand.

4 Nestlé _____ the taste of its Nescafé brand to local tastes.

5 A single centre of _____ can give a company an important competitive advantage.

6 The aim is to develop products which are _____ appealing to different nationalities and cultures.

7 Brands such as Nike are popular in such _____ markets as China and the USA.

8 To market a product _____ , companies often choose to use a global campaign.

2 Complete each sentence with a suitable preposition.

1 Young people find it easy to identify _____ the images portrayed by companies such as Nike.

2 American companies seem to be naturally geared _____ globalisation.

3 Food products are often associated _____ stereotypes from their country of origin.

4 Today's customers are accustomed _____ buying products from all over the world.

5 Many brands are built _____ the use of national stereotypes in their advertising.

6 Most American companies have traditionally treated the whole of Europe _____ a single market.

7 It is difficult to get people to distance themselves _____ local products and cultural values.

3 Match the words with a similar meaning.

1	global	traditional
2	busy	worldwide
3	essential	diverse
4	domestic	hurried
5	cosmopolitan	vital
6	robust	advantageous
7	classic	national
8	beneficial	strong

4 The graph shows the share prices for Microsoft and Apple, July-November 1999. Write a 120-140 word report describing and comparing the share prices.

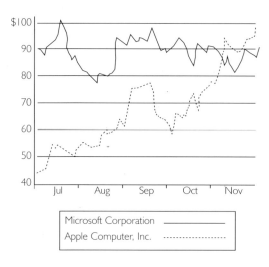

Microsoft Corporation	———————
Apple Computer, Inc.	··················

5 Match the words as they appear in the unit.

1	national	campaign
2	spending	stereotype
3	target	presence
4	global	power
5	creative	market
6	marketing	concept

Inversion

6 Rewrite the sentences beginning with the prompts.

1 We vary both the product and the way it's marketed.
Not only _do we vary the product but also the way it is marketed._

2 Our advertisements aren't usually translated.
Rarely _____

3 It's easier than ever before to advertise globally.
Never _____

4 Cultural differences should never be ignored.
On no account _____

5 We've only had any success with it in Europe.
Only _____

6 Whatever we do, we shouldn't change the logo.
Under no circumstances _____

1 Choose the correct word to fill each gap.

'Buying the market' is an arrangement whereby companies publish component (**1**) _____ and ask pre-qualified vendors to bid for the contract. It is a short-term deal with almost no (**2**) _____ with the supplier and the length of the bidding process is (**3**) _____ by half. Furthermore, the cost of order (**4**) _____ falls to around $5 an order as (**5**) _____ to $50 when it is done on paper. For companies such as aircraft manufacturer Boeing, (**6**) _____ , such an arrangement with its engine suppliers would be unsuitable because of the complex (**7**) _____ between the body of the aircraft and its engines. For companies like Boeing, strategic (**8**) _____ make far more sense because they allow the company to work (**9**) _____ with its supplier, developing the aircraft's engines together. An added (**10**) _____ of this collaboration is that it reduces the financial risks of development programmes.

1	A standards	B specifications	C criteria
2	A exchange	B feedback	C communication
3	A decreased	B reduced	C limited
4	A processing	B developing	C delivering
5	A contrary	B opposed	C different
6	A although	B nevertheless	C however
7	A structure	B interaction	C collaboration
8	A relationships	B alliances	C arrangements
9	A closely	B precisely	C mutually
10	A potential	B satisfaction	C benefit

2 Would you use each of the following suppliers?

1   Using this supplier is unlikely to enhance our image.
2   It's uncertain whether they'll conform to standards.
3   Recent changes have lengthened production cycles.
4   The company has a comprehensive catalogue.
5   Their standard of workmanship is encouraging.
6   Exchange rates would be a factor with this supplier.
7   They fulfil our key selection criteria.
8   Short notice orders might cause potential complications.

3 Match the words with a similar meaning.

1	specification	buildings
2	warranty	measurement
3	attraction	machinery
4	reputation	guarantee
5	plant	incentive
6	premises	image

4 The graph shows unemployment in Italy and Germany, 1993-1998. Write a 120-140 word report comparing unemployment in the two countries.

Percentage of workforce unemployed

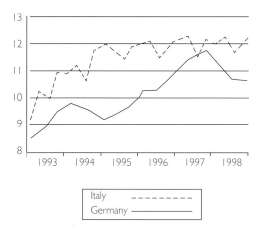

Grammar review

5 Complete the text by choosing the correct options.

An unexpectedly high number of high-profile boardroom changes (**1** *were confirmed/have been confirmed*) by industrial chemicals giant Chemin last week. In addition, the company announced a major reorganisation of (**2** *it's/its*) management structure after the collapse of merger talks with Paintcom, one of (**3** *the/that*) country's largest chemicals companies. Chemin failed (**4** *to win/winning*) support from its shareholders, (**5** *who/which*), according to a company spokesman, (**6** *have been holding out/had been holding out*) right up until the deadline last Monday in the hope of a higher offer.

If the merger (**7** *would have taken place/had taken place*), the deal (**8** *would create/would have created*) the country's largest chemicals company. Although the company (**9** *will not be releasing/will not have released*) details of the planned restructuring until next week at the earliest, the plans (**10** *are likely to/are set to*) involve the disposal of a large proportion of Chemin's assets.

Rumours of several hundred redundancies at Head Office (**11** *also circulated/have also been circulating*) since the company (**12** *announced/has announced*) that a major reorganisation (**13** *will be/would be*) necessary. Not only (**14** *cutbacks are feared/are cutbacks feared*) in the industrial solvents division, but there are also concerns about radical restructuring of the French polishing division. A company spokesman said that staff will be the first to be informed of any reductions as soon as decisions (**15** *are made/will be made*).

Listening Test Part One

- You will hear a sales executive presenting a computer system for electronic meetings.
- As you listen, for questions 1 - 12, complete the notes using up to **three** words or a number.
- You will hear the recording twice.

DecisionMaker® - Solutions for Electronic Meetings

What is DecisionMaker®?

1 DecisionMaker® allows you to hold electronic meetings on _____ .

2 Using computers enables people to express ideas freely without _____ .

Advantages of DecisionMaker®

3 The system generates more ideas by using the _____ of the entire group.

4 The system encourages _____ by keeping the proposer's identity secret.

5 Each idea is judged _____ rather than attitudes towards the proposer.

6 As a result of this team ownership of any proposals made, ideas are _____ , allowing them to be processed more quickly.

7 Equal contributions mean _____ of the meeting by individuals.

8 Automatic documentation means a _____ is not required.

Features of DecisionMaker®

9 The Whiteboard® means that _____ are accessible to the group.

10 FileShare® allows for the _____ within the group.

11 Consensus® offers three possible _____ for indicating opinions.

12 Briefcase® allows you to use your _____ in the meeting.

Listening Test Part Two

- You will hear five different people talking about their jobs.
- For each extract there are two tasks. For Task One, choose the department each speaker works in from the list **A - H**. For Task Two, choose the complaint each speaker makes about a colleague from the list **I - P**.
- You will hear the recording twice.

TASK ONE - DEPARTMENT

- For questions **13 - 17**, match the extracts with the departments, listed **A - H**.
- For each extract, choose the department each speaker works in.
- Write **one** letter **A - H** next to the number of the extract.

13 .....

14 .....

15 .....

16 .....

17 .....

A	legal
B	sales
C	accounts
D	purchasing
E	customer service
F	despatch
G	production
H	personnel

TASK TWO - COMPLAINT

- For questions **18 - 22**, match the extracts with the complaints, listed **I - P**.
- For each extract, choose the speaker's main complaint about a colleague.
- Write **one** letter **I - P** next to the number of the extract.

18 .....

19 .....

20 .....

21 .....

22 ......

I	constant interruptions
J	personal telephone calls
K	untidiness in the office
L	bad time-keeping
M	frequent breaks
N	food in the office
O	gossiping about staff
P	misuse of office equipment

Listening Test Part Three

- You will hear an interview with an HR director about the introduction of a new flexible working scheme.
- For each question **23 - 30**, mark **one** letter **A, B** or **C** for the correct answer.
- You will hear the recording twice.

23 The main reason why ZSV introduced the flexible working scheme was

    A to cope with social changes.

    B to respond to market forces.

    C to integrate new employees.

24 What is the main advantage of the scheme for ZSV?

    A keeping existing staff

    B recruiting new employees

    C reducing the training bill

25 Most staff join the scheme to dedicate more time to their

    A children.

    B hobbies.

    C education.

26 The old scheme was only available to

    A female workers.

    B non-managerial staff.

    C long-term employees.

27 Sally thinks the most popular element of the scheme will be

    A flexible hours.

    B job-sharing.

    C extended leave.

28 Most teleworkers keep in contact by using

    A e-mail facilities.

    B the telephone.

    C video-conferencing.

29 What do managers find most difficult?

    A delegating work

    B keeping motivated

    C managing time

30 Employees are selected for teleworking after an assessment of their

    A home environment.

    B job description.

    C personal qualities.

Reading Test Part Four

- Read the article below about foreign language skills.
- Choose the best word to fill each gap.
- For each question **1 - 10**, mark **one** letter **A**, **B**, **C** or **D**.
- There is an example at the beginning **(0)**.

UK comes bottom of European language league

The United Kingdom has the poorest language skills base in Europe, according to research findings published today. A European Union **(0)** ..... found that UK companies could be losing billions of pounds worth of **(1)** ..... exports due to their poor foreign language skills. Nearly twice as many UK companies **(2)** ..... experiencing difficulties due to language barriers as other European companies. Furthermore, one in eight UK companies thought they had probably missed out on a business **(3)** ..... due to their inability to communicate effectively in an international **(4)** ..... . According to the report, 'Failure to communicate effectively and efficiently with **(5)** ..... export markets in Europe, Latin America and the Asia Pacific region means that for many British firms more than a quarter of their possible revenues are at risk'.

The UK was **(6)** ..... last in a European league table, with only 74 per cent of companies saying they had employees with foreign language skills, compared with 89 per cent in Germany and 84 per cent in France. This is of particular **(7)** ..... to UK exporters, who now ship less than 25 per cent of their total **(8)** ..... to traditionally English-speaking markets. A Government spokesman said that new **(9)** ..... were needed to encourage companies to develop their language skills. 'Many companies come away from negotiations convinced that they have secured a good deal with an overseas client only to find out that the **(10)** ..... they thought they had agreed on are not as profitable as they had hoped.'

Example

0   A   study   B   examination   C   inspection   D   enquiry

A   B   C   D
▬   ▭   ▭   ▭

---

1   A   likely   B   feasible   C   potential   D   conceivable
2   A   announced   B   accounted   C   informed   D   reported
3   A   favour   B   opportunity   C   chance   D   fortune
4   A   scene   B   neighbourhood   C   environment   D   atmosphere
5   A   lucrative   B   fertile   C   beneficial   D   fruitful
6   A   ranked   B   classed   C   graded   D   listed
7   A   distress   B   anxiety   C   worry   D   concern
8   A   commodities   B   holdings   C   goods   D   assets
9   A   ambitions   B   enterprises   C   ventures   D   initiatives
10   A   specifications B   terms   C   conclusions   D   clauses

Tapescripts

Unit 1a: Work roles

Listening

I've just moved from a company with a very strict hierarchy to a fast-growing software company and it's been hard coming to terms with the changes. I mean, don't get me wrong, I enjoy my new job a lot more. I have a lot more responsibility now and everything's done in project teams and managed by objectives. The one thing I do miss, however, is that now, once a project's running, the team's pretty much on its own and left to solve any problems by itself. Before, there was always a superior I could turn to for help, and to be honest, I'd be much happier if that were still the case. Especially when you're starting a new job, having someone to talk to can make things a lot easier.

I produce technical documents, you know, users' manuals and that sort of thing - nothing creative, I'm afraid. Our team's responsible for its own work schedules. And as long as everything's finished before the machine's shipped, it's up to us when we do it. So you'd think with e-mail and everything, we'd all be able to work from home or come and go as we please - but that's not the case. Unfortunately, it's a very conservative company so everyone's still clocking in and out at the same time. I suppose the managers have always worked a routine nine to five and just can't imagine anything else being possible.

I'm an IT consultant and I'm working for a small leisure group on a one-year contract. So I'm travelling around Europe a lot, which I know sounds very glamorous, but it's just a case of jetting in, fixing a hotel's computer and then jetting out again. It also means I'm on call and work very ... shall we say 'flexible' hours, including many weekends. Oh and I'm also responsible for the website, which I work on from home. What I miss is support from colleagues, you know, being able to discuss problems or things like the latest technology with other IT professionals in the same job. So, yes, it's definitely the social side of my job I'd like to improve.

Well, I'm a temp and I'm working as a PA for a law firm in London just now. It's a medium-sized firm that's grown quickly so its organisation is very much like that of a smaller company. OK, I know it's unreasonable to expect a definite job description - I mean, if something needs doing, then I think whoever's available should do it. But I'm already responsible for managing the diaries and correspondence of two senior managers, so when the telephone's ringing all day and people keep asking me to photocopy reports or even make them coffee, it just becomes impossible to get anything done.

I work for the UK subsidiary of a Japanese company and it's very Japanese in terms of the way it's run. I've just got a new boss, who's come over from Japan. We seem to be getting on pretty well at the moment - he always has time for me and gives me lots of support. The only thing is, I don't really have a huge say in what I do - which is all right but sometimes it would be nice to be able to show a bit of initiative. Our work processes are totally standardised as fixed routines, which I don't mind. It's just that I always have to consult him before I can make even the smallest alteration to any job of any sort.

Unit 1b: Company structure

Listening

I = Interviewer   N= Neil

I   So, Neil, why did BT decide to introduce Options 2000?

N   Well, we started looking at flexible working back in 1993. And subsequent staff surveys showed that 96 per cent of our office-based staff wanted to work at home two or three days a week. We thought about how we could respond to this and soon realised that flexible working was very much a win-win-win situation. It's a win for technology, using our own products and practising what we preach. And of course, it reduces BT's office space and cuts costs. But I think the real driver for change was accepting that our people wanted to work differently.

I   Right. And how many of them will actually end up working from home?

N   Our target's 10,000 by the end of the year.

I   10,000!

N   Yes, that's out of about 55,000 office-based staff.

I   And what effect has this had on company structure?

N   Well, the company's been organised around business units for some time now. It used to be very much departmentalised, with work being done in series, you know, passed from one department to the next. But product life cycles are a lot shorter nowadays - for the Internet, say, it's less than 6 months even. So people come together for a specific purpose and then go off to join new projects when the job's done.

I   So, these organisational changes must have had quite an effect on BT's culture.

N   Well, as I said, we've been developing a project-oriented culture. So, people now are paid for what they actually do and not for sitting at a desk from nine to five. But the really fundamental change is that we've become a lot more collaborative, both internally and in our dealings with partners and clients. And people are, of course, now getting used to working on several teams at once, which means they tend to get a lot more variety in their work as well.

I   Yes. And how about the technology? How do you help your teleworkers cope with it?

N   Well, people working from home have, I suppose, had to become more independent about coping with technology. But our corporate intranet is the largest in Europe and we've invested a lot of time and money in making sure there's enough on-line support for anyone using it. Oh, and there is some training available, of course.

I   And what's been the impact so far?

N   Well, it's difficult to say whether productivity's risen or not. But surveys show that since people have had access to work 24 hours a day, they've been working a lot longer days. In fact, we've just implemented a new training programme to help managers recognise this and deal with the situation. Because although some people might produce their best work under this kind of pressure, it's certainly not the case for everyone.

I   Was that one of the challenges when implementing the programme?

N   Yes, as was getting the general concept over. We've also had to adapt to the diversity of our flexible workers. It's not unusual, say, for 400 of them to be on the intranet at midnight.

I   Midnight?

N   Yes.

I   So, what happens when these people need stationery or when their computer crashes?

N   We've had to develop 24-hour, 365-day-a-year support services. I'd say that was probably our toughest challenge, actually.

I   And how have people adapted to working in these virtual teams?

N   Well, so far, very well. New teams usually meet at the start of a project. Of course, you can always find out about the other team members on the company intranet even before you meet them. After the first meeting, most communication is then done by e-mail, so we've had to work out guidelines on how to use e-mail more effectively. At the start we experienced some difficulties with people circulating far too much irrelevant information. And, of course, there's always one or two people who resist any form of change whatsoever.

I   And finally, how do you see the future of the office itself?

N   Well, I think flexible working's bound to increase but there'll always be a place for the office. There'll always be a need for face-to-face contact because even teams working remotely still need to get together every now and again to refocus. Being tied to the desk, *however, is history. In future, mobile personal information systems will have all the tools we need for our jobs. The days of putting bits of paper in drawers are definitely numbered, I'm afraid.*

Unit 2a: Stocks & shares

Listening 1

R = Richard   K= Katie

R   Now, Internet stocks. They were going through the roof earlier this year until they ran into their recent difficulties. So the question is: has the bubble finally burst? Our technology correspondent Katie Johnson joins me in the studio. So Katie, first of all, what drove these prices up so high in the first place?

K   Well, all the hype about the Internet would have attracted some investors looking for a quick profit - but I think the real driving force has been the fact that demand has far exceeded a limited supply. There were only a handful of Internet share offers last year, so opportunities to jump onto the Internet bandwagon have been very limited.

R   And all this is despite the fact they're far from what you'd call a safe investment.

K   Absolutely, yes.

R   But what about good old profits? Do they match the performance of the share prices?

K   Well, this is what's so fascinating. Take Amazon.com, for example, the Internet bookseller. They have a market value of $18bn, turnover in excess of $1bn, and yet they haven't even reached the break-even point. Apart from a couple of companies, such as Yahoo! and America Online, most of them are a long long way away from making any kind of profit whatsoever, never mind the huge profits everyone's hoping for.

R   So why on earth is everyone so keen to invest in them?

K   Well they're very trendy, and of course there's always the brand factor, which is another reason. Companies like Yahoo! and America Online now enjoy incredibly high brand awareness. But the real attraction is the tremendous potential for future revenue, particularly from advertising. Yahoo! already has 144 million page hits a day and nearly 2,000 advertisers. And with Internet usage expected to double within five years, advertising spending is bound to increase.

R   But then how do analysts value these companies?

K   Well, it's not easy. They have few assets in the traditional sense and they all show phenomenal growth in terms of turnover, so analysts are having to rely on alternative yardsticks to compare them.

R   Such as?

K   Such as things like audience reach. Lycos, another search engine like Yahoo!, saw its shares jump by more than a third recently when figures came out saying it reached 45 per cent of all home Internet users.

R   So, let's turn to the recent collapse in these share prices. Has the bubble finally burst?

K   Well, we were due a sell-off, so it's not surprising that shareholders took advantage of the recent sharp rises. But I think what's really depressed prices is the flood of Internet companies that have floated recently and saturated the market with their shares. It seems that supply and demand are now levelling out. In fact, several companies have even seen their shares slide below the offer price. So, yes, enthusiasm does seem to be cooling.

R   Well, it seems to me that anyone investing in Internet shares is in for a bit of a rollercoaster ride. So just why is the market so volatile?

K   Well, it's a very young market, don't forget. And many companies have been listed for only a couple of months. Also, a lot of people who invest in these stocks actually use the Internet to trade on-line. Without the broker's commission, they can afford to buy in and out of stocks several times a day. This makes the market very sensitive to any breaking news. And I think it's this responsiveness which makes it so volatile.

R   So, Katie, the big question. What's the market going to do next?

K   Well, Richard, that's the million dollar question, isn't it? Some of the prices being paid do reflect the value of these companies so I can't really see prices falling much more. And although confidence will return, enthusiasm is cooling so don't expect to see prices soaring in the near future.

R   So how do you see the future for companies in this sector?

K   Well, I think the sector's going to see lots of consolidation activity as the bigger players look to buy talent and market share. Lycos, for example, has just acquired HotBot, one of its rivals. We'll also see one or two large established non-Internet companies looking to enter the market. The giant German publisher Bertelsmann, for example, has just entered into a joint venture with US bookseller Barnes and Noble to challenge Amazon's dominance on the Net. And if the Internet continues to grow like it is, then a few of these companies are bound to see substantial returns on their investments.

Listening 2

R   Now, earlier you mentioned Amazon.com, the Internet bookseller. And I believe you're going to show us a graph illustrating what's been happening to their shares over the last 12 months.

K   Yes, and here it is. Now this example really is typical of what's been happening throughout this whole sector. As you can see, there was a general upward trend in the first six months, with shares going from just $14 to over $100 a share by December last year. But then in January this year, they really took off, soaring to almost $200. Predictably enough, I suppose, investors took advantage of these sharp gains and we saw a sell-off, which meant that by February, Amazon shares had fallen back to their December level again.

R   So, we've seen one sell-off this year already, then?

K   Yes, and that's why I don't think there's any real need to panic about current losses, because as we can see here, there was a very strong recovery and by May, they'd more than doubled in value again, peaking at nearly $220. So, I think the recent losses were fairly predictable. But having said that, the price has collapsed by nearly 50 per cent in the last four weeks. And finally, there we have today's price, down almost $6 at just over $111.

Unit 2b: Mergers & acquisitions

Listening

Good afternoon, ladies and gentlemen. I'm Steve Brown from the Zeneca Public Affairs Department. I'm here today to tell you a little bit more about the merger between Zeneca and the Swedish pharmaceuticals company Astra. So, first of all, the boards of Astra and Zeneca have announced that there is to be an all-share merger of the two companies. The new company will be called AstraZeneca. I'll begin by going through the rationale for the merger and listing some of its benefits. Then I'll go on to give some details about the new board and talk about the financial effects of the merger. And finally, I'll give a brief summary of the terms, including details about dividends and so on.

The merger is a natural step for both partners as they both share the same science-based culture as well as a common vision concerning the future of the industry. The benefits of this move are many. To begin with, the merged group will have an enhanced ability to create long-term growth and increased value for its shareholders. Furthermore, it'll be able to deliver the full potential of its existing and future products through the joint strength and worldwide presence of its global sales and marketing operations. In fact, based on the joint pharmaceutical sales for last year, the AstraZeneca group will be the third largest pharmaceutical company in the world.

The combined strength of the two R&D functions will also ensure an excellent basis for innovation-led growth. With a combined R&D spend of nearly $2bn, AstraZeneca will be one of the largest R&D organisations in the world, which will mean that the company will also be of great interest to academic institutions and biotech companies seeking partners for their research programmes.

At a strategic level, management is hoping that the merger will create sizeable operational efficiencies by restructuring areas of duplication. It has been calculated that synergies resulting from the merger could lead to cost reductions of over a billion dollars within the next three years. Although this sounds like a somewhat optimistic figure, we are quite confident that it can be achieved through streamlining the workforce, particularly in areas like administration and a restructuring of the two sales operations.

Moving on to the board now, the board of AstraZeneca will be drawn equally from the two companies, with Tom McKillop, the Chief Executive, running the company along with his executive team. The board will be headed by Percy Barnevik, the non-executive Chairman, whose job it will be to check that strategy and policy are periodically reviewed and agreement is maintained. The two deputy Chairmen, Sir David Barnes and Håkan Mogren, both have extensive experience of the pharmaceutical industry and business in general. They will be available to advise and support the Chief Executive as necessary.

Unit 3b: Entering a market

Listening

So, what's it like actually doing business with the Chinese? Well, it's difficult to describe because in China there's still no commonly shared perception of what's reasonable or normal in international business, so standards and expectations vary widely from place to place. That's why, when you're doing business in China, it's imperative that you do extensive preparatory work. This means finding out about the particular company, industry, city or region where you're doing business - and not just about the country as a whole.

One of the first things to remember is that the Chinese find it most discourteous if you are late for meetings. It may be, of course, that your first meeting will be in your hotel, but if not, then allow plenty of time for the journey as in most Chinese cities the congestion is every bit as bad as in London. A good tip is to take a business card with the company's address written in Chinese to show the taxi driver. When you get there, you will be greeted by your host, usually a senior manager, and probably some of his or her staff. The visitors will then be ushered into the meeting room.

The leader of your group will be expected to enter first and will generally be offered a seat beside the most senior Chinese person present. This person will usually chair the meeting and act as host and have a translator at his or her side. To begin with, all those present will swap business cards, in itself a very important ceremony, and there will be a short period of small talk. The host will then officially start proceedings with a 'brief introduction' to the Chinese enterprise and its activities. The host may then invite the visiting team to speak. Now at this point it's appropriate for the UK side to begin to make its case. Don't forget to warn your host beforehand if you wish to include any audio-visual aids during this presentation. It's also extremely important that your team should be able to answer any questions on any aspect of your business proposal, your own company and your international competitors.

Following the meeting, the Chinese enterprise will probably arrange a special dinner for the UK guests. Small talk over dinner is essential for relationship-building. For most Chinese, the family counts above all else. It remains the dominant social and political unit in Chinese society so Chinese people will usually be very pleased to be asked about their children and their hopes for their children's future. In social relationships

Chinese people almost always seek to preserve harmony and face. Hosts believe it is their duty to offer their visitors hospitality, even though the visitors themselves may much prefer a day off after intense negotiations. It's very common, for instance, for the host enterprise to organise sightseeing trips for its guests and it would, of course, be a discourtesy not to accept these invitations.

Unit 4a: The future of work

Listening

I = Interviewer   J = Jan Dunn

I   So Jan, why did BA decide to move to Waterside?

J   Well, we had a lot of people scattered about in a lot of different buildings. British Airways has been around a long time so we've inherited a lot of old offices and buildings. Leases were running out on a lot of key buildings on the Heathrow site and we decided that rather than try to renew them, it would make more sense for us financially to build a new building on this site. So although it was a £200m project, it was, in fact, a cost-effective move for BA.

I   But why such a radically different building? What was the main objective?

J   Well, we knew from opinion surveys that our work environment needed improving. When designing the building, we very much wanted to realise a vision which was team-based and spaced, one that involved bringing people together in an open working environment. We now have an excellent facility where people can meet and work anywhere in the building. And by centralising our information and data, we can now work together much more effectively than before. We also looked at informality and ways of reducing hierarchy.

I   Such as?

J   Physically, we used to have a very hierarchical set-up. PAs, for example, used to sit right outside the manager's office and we questioned whether that kind of system really helped the way we worked. We also looked at things like the size and purpose of office space. And we made small changes like not allocating executive parking.

I   So, how is the building laid out?

J   Right, the building itself was designed around a village structure. What we've got is a central street with six houses coming off it. It's designed so residents, that's the people who work here, park in a secure area beneath the building and then come up through the street. This means they have to walk through the street to get to their place of work, wherever that might be that day. And the idea there was very much, and it does work, that we would all be very visible and we would stop and talk or bump into each other at the shop or the bank. So, again, everyone, whatever their level, comes through the building the same way.

I   So, if someone can be working anywhere in the building, how do you find them?

J   It's very simple. All the phones in the building are dumb terminals. So, wherever I am in the building, I can log into the system as 95001, which activates that particular terminal and directs all my calls to it. So I'm always 95001, whether I'm in the building or even at home. We also have voice mail and an electronic diary system just in case people are unavailable. And obviously there are maps in the street and information points as well.

I   Going back to the street for a moment, I noticed there are lots of high street facilities. What was the thinking behind that?

J   Well, it's very clear that people need to do things like pop to the bank or pick up shopping or whatever. Normally if you want to do those things, you're going to have to dash out at lunchtime or after work. So what we've done is identify what people need to do and we've just made them available on site. It's a convenience thing, that's all.

I   Oh right. Yes, that's handy. Now I believe you've also looked at changing the meetings culture.

J   Yes, we're encouraging people on the classics really: making sure you need a meeting and that you're inviting the right people. I suppose we're suggesting that we wouldn't expect a useful meeting to be bigger than say 20 people. But we've got a lot of flexibility. I can choose a location suited to the type of meeting I want to run. There's everything from the cafés and informal meeting rooms right up to the theatre, which seats 400 people.

I   So what difference has Waterside made to your typical day?

J   Right, well, first thing in the morning I have a choice of whether I come into Waterside or not because I've got a laptop and access to the computer network from home or from other sites. So what I've tended to do is try and book meetings all on the same day if I can as it cuts down my travelling time basically. And if I do come into Waterside, I've just got more options. I really feel I get things done quicker and more effectively and that I'm making better use of my time.

Unit 4b: e-business

future perfect
future continuous

Listening

Well, it's already made a huge impact and by the time the project's fully implemented, we'll have networked over 300,000 employees and suppliers – they'll all be able to communicate through e-mail. And it's this interconnectivity, it's changing everything about the way we work. I mean, last year around 15 per cent of our in-service staff development was carried out through Web-based distance learning using the company intranet. And we reckon that for every 1,000 days of classroom-based teaching that's supplied by distance learning, it generates about $500,000 in efficiency gains. And this year, we'll be delivering up to 30 per cent of our courses by distance learning. So we'll be looking at savings of over $100 million.

We're one of the largest insurance organisations in Canada, offering a wide range of financial products. We rely on a system of independent agents to distribute our products so it's really important to maintain a close relationship with them. This used to be done over the telephone but that was all very time-consuming for our employees and meant we could only supply agents with information during office hours. Now we have the extranet, which means that all our representatives can keep in touch around the clock and get the latest information about offerings. They can also request back-up articles and information such as telemarketing scripts and advertisements. And of course, we'll be introducing more and more new product lines so it's essential that our agents get the back-up they need.

We're one of the Netherlands' leading banks with 1,300 branches here and abroad. We deal with both businesses and consumers but our primary focus is small and medium-sized businesses - SMBs as we call them. As part of our offering to SMBs, we recently launched a Web-based euro project which provides free briefings to both customers and staff about the new European currency. Since the issues surrounding the euro will constantly be changing, people will need regular updating. By providing up-to-the-minute bulletins, we're establishing ourselves as a major player in the Eurozone countries. This, in turn, is enhancing our clients' perceptions of us and strengthening our customer base.

Well, we are one of France's most prestigious bicycle manufacturers, selling mainly to professionals and people with a real passion for cycling as a sport. The best bit about our new website is that it lets customers actually design their own personalised cyber cycle. All they have to do is choose a basic model and then decide what frame, wheels, pedals, colour and so on they want. They pay on-line by credit card and the bike is then delivered to their nearest dealer within 14 days. It's as simple as that. Our business was initially aimed at mostly French customers but with the new

way of using the Internet, we have been able to create an international presence at a fraction of what it would have cost to advertise outside the domestic market.

After recent restructuring we felt we needed to change the company culture to reflect our leaner structure. Processes that used to be highly bureaucratised needed to be simplified. One area we really had to tackle was procurement. After filling in massive amounts of paperwork, getting requisite signatures and then faxing orders off, our employees sometimes had to wait over a month for things like office material and PCs to get here. A real advantage with the new system is there's less margin for error because if the form isn't filled in correctly, then the system says so immediately. So less time'll be wasted on sorting out problems. By the end of the year, we'll have reduced our paper invoices from five million to zero.

Unit 4: Exam practice (Exam focus audio cd)

Listening Test Part One

Good morning and welcome to Eldertree Cosmetics. My name's Maria Darcy and I'm the Managing Director. I'm here today to tell you a little bit about the history of the company before you're taken on the official tour.

So, Eldertree Cosmetics was founded by Olivia Jenkins in 1975 originally under the name of Eldertree Cottage. And in those days it really was very much a cottage industry with Olivia and her husband Mike producing a range of natural soaps in their own kitchen. The soaps proved to be a recipe for success and sales took off due to the popularity of simple, chemical-free products. It soon became clear, though, that Olivia and Mike would be unable to satisfy demand if they continued working out of their kitchen. So in 1977 Mike began searching for suitable premises and this resulted in the move to the Old Bakery in the town centre.

At the start of the next decade sales continued to grow dramatically and Olivia and Mike widened their product range to enter new markets such as haircare and cosmetics. This led to rapid expansion and a change of name to Eldertree Cosmetics. It was at this point that Olivia and Mike realised they needed support with their sales and marketing efforts. So they took on an experienced Sales Manager, who was able to win substantial contracts with some of the largest UK cosmetics retailers.

This significant increase in business meant that Eldertree needed to recruit a lot more staff and upgrade its facilities. The company had reached a critical point. In order to develop, it required the resources and knowledge that only a large and established organisation could offer. And faced with several takeover bids, Olivia and Mike finally decided that in the interests of Eldertree and its employees, they would sell the company to the UK's biggest high-street chemist, Greenaway, which they did in 1987.

Greenaway's first move was to look at ways of increasing productivity. Although the Old Bakery site had been upgraded over the years, it was still limited by its size and layout. So in 1988 Greenaway began construction of the new factory, which was completed at the end of the following year. The other major decision which was taken at this time was to continue to trade under the Eldertree brand name and not that of its parent company.

Today Eldertree Cosmetics is a state-of-the-art producer of high-quality cosmetic products. Structural changes have seen certain functions move to Greenaway's Head Office. By moving its marketing operations to Greenaway, for example, Eldertree has not only cut costs, but also enjoyed the advantages of its parent's substantial advertising budget. And I'm sure you're all familiar with the new TV campaign. Despite the fact that Eldertree has grown enormously, it still retains a family atmosphere, with many of the original employees from the Old Bakery still working for the company today. Over the last ten years or so, these loyal employees have seen the Eldertree name successfully establish itself as a market leader in both the UK and overseas.

On that note, I'd like to hand you over to Samantha Eagle, our PR Manager, who'll be conducting your tour of the factory today.

Listening Test Part Two

Well, I guess on the whole it was quite interesting talking about setting and meeting objectives and co-ordinating projects. It's just that I'd hoped we'd learn more practical things like how to motivate groups and manage conflict and make group communication more effective. Anyway, I was pretty tired by the end of the day and I got in quite late because the centre was a long way from home. But that in itself wasn't really a problem. I think one day would have been more than enough. I didn't really understand why they needed two whole days. It wasn't that expensive though, so I'm hoping I'll be allowed to go on another course soon. There are some good writing skills courses around, I believe.

I feel a lot more confident now having done the course. The trainer gave us some really great tips on preparing more effectively. And I also got to see myself on video. There I was talking about our latest product when most of the time I was standing in front of the screen. So no-one in the audience could see my nice OHTs anyway. We certainly didn't have any complaints about the price even though it was pretty expensive. But I can't understand why they held it in Newcastle. It took me half the day to get there and I was exhausted before the course even started. We really should have found somewhere closer to the office.

I had a great time. We did lots of role-plays, mainly about delegating or dealing with interruptions, which I really enjoyed. And I think it must have done me some good. Even my boss has noticed that I'm getting better at prioritising my workload. And this week I managed to get my report in before the deadline for a change. There must have been about twenty of us by the time all the latecomers had arrived, which was about right for the group dynamics. The only thing that I'd change would be the refreshments. You'd have thought they could have provided more than just a salad for lunch, wouldn't you? It wasn't even particularly fresh either.

Originally, I'd wanted to do the effective negotiations course. But my boss told me this course would be more useful. You know what I'm like. Even when I don't want to do something, I end up saying yes. Even now I still find it difficult to say 'no', but at least this course has made me more confident about trying to stick up for myself. We covered a lot of stuff. But of course you can't expect the trainer to do everything in just six sessions, can you? So we had to miss out on some really interesting topics. I was a bit disappointed, for example, that we didn't do anything on body language.

The programme itself looked really interesting, which is why I went for this course rather than the assertiveness training one. And I guess we did have a few useful topics like writing minutes and preparing agendas. And we started looking at roles, especially the role of the chairperson. But all in all, it was really disappointing and so chaotic. We never really knew what we were supposed to be doing. But then the tutor didn't seem to know either. She kept taking calls on her mobile during the sessions and I wouldn't be surprised if it was someone phoning her to tell her what to do next! Good job it didn't cost too much. Otherwise we'd have been asking the centre for our money back.

Listening Test Part Three

S = Sue   P = Peter

S   *And today on Business Spot we have this year's winner of 'South-East Company of 1999', Peter Jones, Manager of corporate travel agency Corporate Direct. Hello Peter. And congratulations on your award.*
P   *Thank you, Sue.*
S   *So, Peter, how has the award affected your company so far?*
P   *Well, Sue, we've been stunned by all the media attention, which might even generate some new business, you never know. But the real benefit is the boost to morale. Everyone's been working extremely hard to make the business a success and it's great to see their efforts rewarded.*

S   *So why did you start Corporate Direct?*
P   *Well, about six years ago I was made redundant. I couldn't really see myself working for any of the local travel agencies. And I'd always wanted to do my own thing. So I decided it was now or never.*
S   *What did your wife think?*
P   *She wasn't too keen initially. She didn't want me turning her home into a travel agency. But thankfully it wasn't long before we could open a small office.*
S   *And business is still booming. Some of your services are expanding very rapidly.*
P   *Yes, they are. Core services like car rental were popular right from the word go, although what's really taken off is our monthly journal Travel Direct. Subscriptions are increasing at ten to twenty per cent a month. We're also looking at ways of promoting our currency exchange service.*
S   *So things are obviously going very well for you. But what exactly makes Corporate Direct so unique?*
P   *Well, although there are two other independent travel offices here in the area, offering people the same unbiased advice, as far as I know, we're still the only company keeping a comprehensive database of clients' travel guidelines, things like which airlines they use ...*
S   *... meaning you make arrangements in line with each company's policies ...*
P   *Yes, that's right. And like the other big names, we can also provide very competitive rates too.*
S   *And as I understand it, you've also been developing the consultancy arm of the company as well. What services do you currently offer?*
P   *Well, advising companies on their travel policies is a very popular service and one which looks set to develop even further. What really attracts companies, though, is our corporate hospitality consultancy. We advise people on all sorts of PR type things, everything from wine-tasting to car-racing. We've also seen an increase in the number of clients asking our advice on language training courses.*
S   *But why does a company use an agency rather than make its own arrangements? Wouldn't it be cheaper?*
P   *Well, some companies do of course arrange things themselves. And in some cases it may indeed be cheaper for them to do so. But what's most important for companies, though, is that by using a corporate travel agency, they get everything arranged far more quickly, without the hassle of dealing with numerous providers. And I suppose our clients appreciate not having to worry about quality. Quite simply, we take the stress out of organising corporate travel.*
S   *So, who are your biggest clients?*
P   *Well, there's quite a range. We've got clients in the retail industry, like fashion companies, for example, and we're seeing far more interest from hotels and catering companies. Although, in general, I'd say our customers are more often than not from accountancy firms or banks and I can't see that changing in the future.*
S   *Speaking of the future, what new ventures are planned for Corporate Direct?*
P   *Well, we're introducing a 24-hour emergency service in the next two to three months. Clients will be able to call our Hotline for help at any time.*
S   *I should imagine that'll be really useful.*
P   *Well, we hope so. But our biggest priority at the moment is updating our Internet site in time for the Travel Fair in a fortnight's time. Clients will be able to access our website and book services directly from our home page. We're also considering introducing a Corporate Direct Credit Card, which will let clients settle their accounts with us on a monthly basis. But let's just say that's not exactly going to happen tomorrow.*
S   *Well, I'm afraid we'll have to finish there. Thank you Peter for talking to us today and congratulations again on your award.*

> **Exam focus: Speaking Test contains mock interviews.**
> **No tapescript is provided.**

Unit 5a: Staff motivation

Listening

Well, I've only been here a few months but I feel as if I've fitted in quite well so far. Everyone seems to have time to talk to me when I need help, which I really appreciate. The work's beginning to get interesting too. It's just that by now, I feel I really should be getting up to speed. Only it's a relatively new position and nobody's really spelt out what the exact scope of the job is or what my responsibilities and priorities should be. I think my line manager needs to give me a more concrete idea of what she expects me to achieve. She's back from holiday next week so maybe we could sit down together then.

Well, I get the feeling that we're starting to fall a bit behind other companies. I mean, when you look in the papers, you can't help noticing there's a bit of a gap between ourselves and the current going rate. I mean, it's not that I'm unhappy here or anything. I really like my job - it's interesting work and I think it's great that the job's so flexible. It's just that, at the end of the day, nobody likes to feel undervalued, do they? And in my position, it's not just myself I've got to think about. I've got responsibilities outside work as well.

Well, it's great to be part of a successful team. I don't think you could wish for harder-working or more dedicated colleagues. But I just sometimes think that our efforts aren't always rewarded. I know different managers have different styles but, well, everyone likes to feel appreciated, don't they? I mean, in my last job, managers always made a point of praising us when we beat our targets. One manager even used to encourage us to clap and cheer each other. And I must admit, I do miss that at times. I find praise here is sometimes a bit, shall we say, limited. It's like there's a 'That's what you're paid for' type of attitude.

I suppose, on the whole, I've got very little to complain about really. I get on with the rest of the team and that kind of thing. But there's one thing that's been on my mind for a while now. I just feel that, well, I've reached a stage where I'm capable of dealing with a lot more responsibility than I do at present. I just don't feel stretched any more. I don't feel as though I'm contributing as much as I could. It's almost as if I'm on autopilot. Things are beginning to feel a bit stale. What I need is a bit of variety, something to get my teeth into - a challenge.

Well, you're probably already aware of the fact that things aren't functioning too smoothly in Production at the moment. I don't know what other people have said but personally I think it's down to our procedures. There's no formal system for putting our ideas forward and in the past suggestions have just been ignored. I think management has to accept a lot of the responsibility. What we need to do is schedule regular meetings, which will improve the flow of information in both directions. I mean, at the moment I get more information through the shop floor grapevine than from my line manager.

Unit 5b: Recruitment

Listening

Good afternoon. My name's Guy Kirkwood and I'm here to tell you a little bit today about how the executive search process works. Now in Europe the executive search industry is worth $10bn a year, with a lot of that business being conducted in the UK. UK recruiters basically use one of four methods: there's agency recruitment, advertising selection (which is advertising in newspapers), a combination of selection and search and, at the top-end, executive search, otherwise known as headhunting. The executive search market is particularly prevalent in areas where market growth has been driven by skills shortages in client companies who are in a constant process of change. This is particularly the case in the finance, consulting and IT sectors, for example.

There is a fairly standard operating procedure for the delivery of headhunting assignments. It begins with a client giving a headhunter exclusive instruction and a brief to fill a vacancy. The headhunter's first task is to target potential companies, then individuals within those companies, either through desk research or through extensive contact networks. The headhunter then speaks to those individuals who match the specified criteria closely and are most appropriate for the job in question.

The headhunter then meets a number of potential candidates, either at their own offices or at a neutral location. Of course, these meetings have to be arranged and held with the utmost discretion. The headhunter then puts together the curriculum vitaes and presents his findings to the client. At this meeting the client is given a shortlist of about eight candidates and selects three or four of them for interview. This number gives a good chance of a successful candidate being hired. The candidates then go through the client's own interview procedure, possibly along with other candidates that applied directly to the company in response to an advertisement. Afterwards, the headhunter gives professional advice to both sides and facilitates the offer process to make sure that the whole assignment ends with a successful hire.

As for remuneration, the headhunter will receive a proportion, usually about 30 per cent, of the first annual salary of the person appointed. When a search company has been given an exclusive instruction to fill a vacancy, payment is normally billed in three instalments: first of all a retainer, then a second instalment upon submission of the shortlist and finally, a completion fee when the appointee starts with the client.

Now the advantage of a good headhunter is that he can provide a clear understanding of the business environment, a client's activities, their strengths and weaknesses and those of their rivals. This kind of comprehensive information can only be obtained through painstaking detective work, a close relationship with the key players in the industry and an international presence.

Headhunting is considered by many to be a 'black art' at best, unethical at worst. Yet at its highest levels, search is time and cost-efficient and provides a client with commercially sensitive information which would be otherwise unavailable. It targets those people who are happy in their current position, motivated and able to consistently deliver top performance - in other words, just the people who can benefit the client's growth plans and who cannot be accessed in any other way.

Model answers to Ex ❸, page 84 (Exam focus audio cd)

5b One-minute talk: How to fill a key vacancy

In order to fill a key vacancy, a company will usually follow the same standard procedure.

It will begin by producing an accurate job description of what it would like the successful candidate to do. From this, it can then produce a profile of this ideal candidate, which is a list of skills, experience, attributes and so on.

Having produced this profile, the company must then decide on the best recruitment method to capture a candidate with this profile. This might be an internal advertisement or an external advertisement in a newspaper, on the Internet say, even an agency or perhaps a headhunter.

Having decided on the best recruitment method, the advertisements are then placed or the headhunter contacted and a list of candidates will be then drawn up to be put through the company's recruitment processes. This might be interviews, psychometric tests or even hand-writing analysis. This will then produce the ideal candidate for the company.

The company will then have to negotiate terms with this candidate and, hopefully, this will result in terms which are both affordable for the company and attractive enough to get the candidate they want.

Well, in my opinion, you can never under-estimate the importance of having a good CV.

In the majority of cases, your CV is the employer's first impression of you, your first chance to impress your potential employer, let's say. It is the essential illustration of your suitability for the job, showing how your skills and experience match your employer's requirements.

But more than that, it shows your ability to summarise, prioritise and present information effectively, essential skills in today's job market. It also shows your linguistic and communicative abilities.

Even though employers these days use a variety of selection techniques, such as analysing your handwriting, a good CV is still the single most important part of any application.

Unit 6a: Corporate culture

Listening 1

I = Interviewer   G= Göran Nilsson

I   And now to IKEA. The Swedish furniture retailer has just reported turnover of 56 billion Swedish kroner from its 150 stores worldwide. Now, IKEA puts its success down to corporate culture. So with me today to explain the secret of IKEA's culture is Managing Director of IKEA UK, Göran Nilsson. Good morning, Mr Nilsson.

G   Good morning.

I   Now is every IKEA store really exactly the same?

G   Well, in terms of culture they're pretty well uniform. Although our culture will naturally bond with the local culture to some extent, our core values such as simplicity and cost-consciousness are valid in all cultures. So we don't need to adapt the way we operate to run our stores. And as for products, although we make some minor adaptations to suit local tastes, we produce exactly the same catalogue in all 28 countries.

I   And where do these values originate?

G   It all goes back to Sweden in the 50s and 60s. IKEA's founder, Ingvar Kamprad, started the company at a time of democratic and social change ...

I   Are IKEA's values those of its founder, then?

G   Well, they have evolved over the last 57 years, of course, but I think our mission statement 'A better life for the majority of people' still very much reflects the spirit of those early years. Having said that though, I think Ingvar's ability to relate to a co-worker in China today would be pretty limited, though.

I   You mentioned China. How does IKEA cope with such diversity amongst its employees?

G   Well, funnily enough, I've been working for IKEA for 15 years in Sweden, Italy, Canada, the USA and what's struck me most is how much we have in common. People may interpret certain concepts such as responsibility and freedom differently but our core values such as humbleness exist in every country.

I   So, what are the advantages of such a strong corporate culture?

G   They're tremendous. For one, there's a real bond between our operations around the world. It's easy to transfer across borders because you know the values will be exactly the same. And from a marketing and positioning point of view it's very advantageous as well. But the real pay-off is that it makes IKEA unique. You can clone our products and our store concept but not our culture. It takes years to build and it has to be maintained daily.

I   But how do you educate 40,000 workers?

G   We begin by making sure people understand the values. That's why the IKEA Way seminars are so vital. All managers attend them and then it's their responsibility to pass the message on. Corporate culture also figures in meetings ...

I   Do you use educational videos and brochures as well?

G   Videos and brochures are helpful tools but only if used in conjunction with 'walking the talk' and discussing values with management. We have various initiatives which regularly provide co-workers with the opportunity to participate and contribute to these discussions.

I   So, does culture affect IKEA's recruitment process?

G   It has a major impact. Although it's important for us to get highly-skilled people into the company, we're not interested if there's a conflict of value systems. Anyone expecting a flash car or status symbols has no future with us. Recruitment at IKEA's an extensive process, based on judgements about a candidate's value systems and attributes. We can add retail skills, no problem, but it's tough to change someone's mindset.

I   Does that go for career advancement too?

G   Yes, it does.

I   So Swedish managers will always have more chance of promotion then?

G   We find that many Scandinavians identify more easily with our culture but there is no written or unwritten rule concerning the nationality of senior managers. It would be impossible, however, for anyone to advance within IKEA without wholly understanding and buying into the company's philosophy and culture. So managers are encouraged to visit Sweden and learn the language etc. and management inductions include at least one week in Almhult, where the company began.

I   And finally, Ingvar Kamprad stepped down as President in the mid-80s, replaced by Anders Moberg. What effect did this have on the development of IKEA's culture?

G   Both Moberg and our current Chief Executive, Anders Dahlvig, worked closely with Kamprad for many years and have a deep knowledge and understanding of Kamprad's original vision and philosophy. Naturally, IKEA is different today than it was 10 years ago, primarily because it is three times bigger and has entered many more diverse and challenging markets. But our values and mission - to provide quality, affordable products for the majority of people - remain very much in situ.

Listening 2

Speaker 1

We organise anti-bureaucrat weeks, where all the managers have to work in the store showrooms, warehouses or restaurants for at least one week a year. The managers also have to work very hard at IKEA. In fact, the pace is such that we sometimes joke about 'management by running around'.

Speaker 2

The company's very informal. We dress casually and believe in a relaxed, open-plan office atmosphere. In countries like Germany and France, for example, we use informal terms of address such as 'du' and 'tu' rather than 'Sie' and 'vous'. But this kind of environment actually puts pressure on management to perform because there's no security available behind status or closed doors.

Speaker 3

Ingvar constantly bypassed formal structures to talk directly with front-line managers. And whenever he visited a store, he tried to meet and shake hands with every employee, offering a few words of praise, encouragement or advice as he did so.

Speaker 4

Our entire East European strategy was mapped out by Ingvar on a small paper napkin. Just about every aspect of the entry strategy was laid out on this small piece of paper - we call it his Picasso. And for the past few years we've just built on and expanded that original version.

Speaker 5

There's also the story about Ingvar driving around town late one night checking out hotel prices till he found one economical enough. I've no idea whether it's true or not but I guess it's all part of the aura and the legend surrounding the man.

Unit 7a: Industrial espionage

Listening 1

J = Jill   O = Oliver   R = Rick

J   Good morning. Sorry I'm a little late. How did the board meeting go yesterday?

O   I didn't know there was a board meeting planned for yesterday.

R   There wasn't. It was an emergency meeting.

O   Emergency? Sounds exciting. What's the problem?

R   That's what we're here to talk about this morning. Close the door, would you Jill?

J   Yes, of course.

R   Thanks. Right, as you may know, we've lost several major contracts this year to Centronics, our biggest rival. Each time they've targeted the customer just as their contracts were up for renewal.

J   Are you saying they've somehow got access to our files?

R   Well, one of our customers was still loyal enough to inform us that Centronics seemed to have good information about the terms and conditions of their contract with us.

O   But surely, you don't think that someone's passing on that kind of information?

R   We don't know. That's the problem. And that's what we've got to find out. If there genuinely is a problem, then we'll have to find out whether Centronics has infiltrated us or whether it's an inside job. So, we need to look at our systems and our people - and that's why you're both here.

Listening 2

O   So, what did you have in mind, Rick?

R   Well, first of all, Oliver, could someone have hacked into our intranet from outside?

O   Hack into the intranet? I doubt it. We've got pretty up-to-date security on the system.

J   Which means it's probably an inside job, right? Any ideas who it might be?

R   If I knew that, we wouldn't be here. So, we'll need to check out everyone who's joined us in the last 12 months.

J   The last 12 months? You don't think Centronics has placed a spy here, do you?

R   I'm not sure what to think, Jill. But we should check out their CVs anyway.

J   But it'll take ages if we do that. Besides, their references would have been checked at the time anyway.

R   I know, but what about their previous employers? Were they checked?

J   Well ... we ... we don't normally ...

R   Exactly. I think it'd also be a good idea if you looked back at your appraisal records. See if you can find anyone who's disgruntled or making noises about wanting more money ...

J   Do you mean for the whole company or just Sales?

R   Well, start with Sales and then keep looking if you don't find anything. We've got to be thorough on this one. The board's taking it very seriously. Oliver, on the systems side of things, what can we do?

O   Well, I guess the first thing is to look at access. You know, see who's got access to what information.

R   Could you report back to me on that as soon as possible?

O   Sure. And I suppose I could also issue individual passwords so ...

R   That's true. And then we'd know exactly who was logging on, wouldn't we?

O   And what they were looking at - and when they were logging on.

J   How about e-mail? Can we check people's e-mail?

O   No problem, it's all automatically archived on the server. I'll get print-outs for you, Rick.

J   And if I could see them, too, I could see who's dissatisfied and have a look at their appraisal notes and their personal record file.

O   OK.

J   That way I should be able to get an idea as to whether anyone's bearing a grudge.

O   Good idea, Jill. OK, do that. But make sure you do it discreetly. If word got out about this, then whoever's doing it would stop and destroy the evidence.

J   That's true. It wouldn't do much for morale either.

O   Which is already low enough around here at the moment.

R   Yes, this isn't exactly what we needed right now, is it?

J   What if we don't come up with anything, what are we going to do then?

R   The board's thinking about bringing in a security consultant. She'd pose as a temp in the Sales Department - you know, talk to people and get the gossip, find out who's unhappy and that kind of thing.

J   But I don't see the point. How would she be able to find out anything that we couldn't?

O   And it'd certainly go down well in Sales if they found out about it.

R   Yes, well ... Let's just hope it doesn't come to that.

Unit 7b: Business ethics

Listening

I suppose, in a way, it's a kind of generation thing. When George started, there was no such thing as political correctness in the office environment. In those days, I'm sure it was common practice to call colleagues 'love' or 'darling', pay compliments about their figures or even give them gifts and things. But you just can't do that nowadays and he should have known better. He says his secretary never complained about it to him in person and that if she had, he'd have stopped doing it, but she didn't. Instead, she went straight to the board and warned them that she'd take legal action if nothing was done about it. Well, they soon hauled George in and explained the situation. George was outraged and told them what they could do with the job there and then.

If you'd looked around the workplace, I guess you would have seen the evidence. I mean, in a company of this size you would have expected to see at least some ethnic diversity in the workplace, wouldn't you? Anyway, someone finally discovered a secret file with all the applicants who were not given an interview. Whoever it was blew the whistle to the local press and that was it - the company was faced with a PR disaster and a police investigation. Of course, the first thing the board did was give the well-paid HR executive his marching orders and insist that it was his prejudice and not company policy. But if that was the case, then why hadn't they noticed what was going on?

I'm sure Sharleen didn't think she was doing anything wrong at the time. She'd been told to put together a report on the market penetration of a new safety product we'd just launched. So she had to find out how much business our main rival was doing. OK, so hacking into their corporate intranet wasn't the right way of going about it - but no-one realised she was a complete whizzkid. Luckily, they didn't find out what happened. If they had, it would have cost us a fortune. You can imagine everyone's reaction when she announced what she'd done. Our Ethics Officer went mad and had to quickly put together an official code for dealing with competitors. As for Sharleen, well, she just got away without even so much as an official warning!

We'd been doing business with them for years and our sales executives had always enjoyed very good relationships with them. I don't think for one minute it would have made any difference if we hadn't offered them the occasional thank you for their business. But we always thought of it as good customer relationship management. What's wrong with the odd weekend away for a loyal customer? Anyway, the new CEO changed all that. Maybe it was a cultural thing, I don't know, but she suspended all freebies pending a review. She also recruited someone to regulate dealings with our clients - a sort of moral policeman, I guess. She even wrote to all our customers warning them not to accept any kind of presents from any of our reps.

Every business wants to be ethically sound but it's a hyper-competitive world out there and when you're under pressure to make money and keep to a budget, it's a different matter. Pete, the Production Manager, didn't like the new regulation spray paint - it just wasn't as good - so he carried on using the old stuff. He knew there'd be trouble if anyone found out. But I guess he just hoped they wouldn't. Of course, some campaigners tested the local water and found evidence of the banned chemicals. I suppose when you think about the PR nightmare that followed and the hefty fine the company had to pay, Pete was lucky to get away with just a letter threatening dismissal if he used the old paint ever again.

Model answers to Ex ❹, page 110 (Exam focus audio cd)

7b One-minute talk: How to encourage ethical behaviour from employees

Figures show that more and more companies are now reporting their ethical performance and it's clear I think that companies now have to address the issue of ensuring ethical behaviour amongst their staff. The question is of course - how?

To begin with, awareness is key. The company needs to set out an official code of ethical practice and ensure that all employees have access to it and can understand it easily. The company then needs to implement an effective and anonymous system of reporting any breaches of this code. Once these procedures are in place, the company can then benchmark its ethical practice against those of industry leaders and see how it's doing. I think it's also vital that companies ensure that their senior managers set a good example, 'walk the talk' so to speak. If they don't behave ethically why should staff?

And finally, the company needs to put ethics high on the training and staff development agenda. It needs to make staff understand why ethics is important not just to the company but also to them as well.

7b One-minute talk: The importance of ethics in today's business world

Well, today globalisation is allowing companies to source from ever greater distances. This enables a company to exploit the economic advantages of low labour costs in one country and high market value in another.

Of course, they have to be careful not to be seen to be exploiting the workers. Consumers are becoming ever more sensitive to the exploitation stories and indeed environmental issues. This is because as consumers become richer and become used to spending more on a product, they also feel that they should be spending ethically. This is backed up by media stories and press items, and exploitation stories receive very good press. And of course, they can cause great damage. The bigger the brand, the higher the risk of a PR disaster.

Also companies are now having to worry about PR among their own employees. After all, recent stories about fat cat executive salaries can easily affect morale and thus workers' productivity.

Unit 8a: Global brands

Model answers to Ex ❸, page 118 (Exam focus audio cd)

8a One-minute talk: The importance of a global presence

With more mergers and acquisitions than ever before, I think it's becoming quite clear that a company in the future will need to have a global presence in order to compete in tomorrow's market place. This presence can give a company many competitive advantages.

To begin with, say, it can give access to local market knowledge, which can

avoid some very, very expensive mistakes on account of cultural conflicts. Once more, it can spread the risk of doing business. If a company sells to more than one market, it can survive a downturn in any one of those markets, that's quite clear. And if a company becomes truly global, it can move its production around from country to country and take advantage of the best conditions at any given time. And the size of the company means it can realise economies of scale in advertising or distribution or shipping, for example.

So I think, all in all, when these things are taken into consideration, it's quite clear that any company not looking to establish a global presence in future may not have a future.

8a One-minute talk: How to promote an imported brand

With so many people these days making a conscious decision to buy domestic products, the pressure on those companies wishing to promote imported brands is greater than ever before.

Initially, a company needs to show how their product is superior to the local equivalents. Maybe it's better quality; maybe it's more stylish. A company needs to show customers the benefits of being more adventurous in their buying decisions to encourage them to move away from the current products they use. If you market a product as something exotic or unusual, you're bound to attract new clients. Cultural stereotypes are also a powerful selling tool. A cosmetics range associated with French chic, for example, is bound to attract customers. And if people are looking to buy a reliable car, there's no better label than 'made in Germany'. These national associations can also be exploited at the point of sale. Playing French music in supermarkets, for example, is proven to improve the sales of French wine.

Basically, if you want to successfully promote an imported brand, you need to give your customers a good reason to try something a little bit more exciting than their own home brands.

8a One-minute talk: The importance of stereotypes in advertising

Well, stereotypes are useful to advertisers because they're basically a shorthand. You've got thirty seconds to get your main selling point across. And with a stereotype you can establish a theme in two.

A stereotype is consistent and easily identifiable to a whole national group. When a German audience see a Scotsman in a kilt, they instantly know that the ad is going to be about economy. And they can make us feel good about our own value systems or customs. We might pit a refined Englishman against a brash New Yorker and that'll give the impression that the product we're selling is obviously full of taste and discretion. And of course, in this way, stereotypes are often identified with positive qualities. For example, the German Audi designers in white lab coats are obviously obsessed with perfection. And so we can guarantee that any product we buy from them is going to be designed to perfection.

And lastly, stereotypes make good comedy because everybody wants to laugh at other countries and people who are different. And of course, if they've had a laugh, they're more likely to remember the advert.

Unit 8b: Global sourcing

Listening

I = Interviewer   C = Craig

I   We keep hearing all about the globalisation of markets and supply chains and so on but why has global sourcing suddenly become so widespread?

C   Well, I think there are several factors, really. I mean, as companies expand internationally their outlook becomes increasingly global. What's more, hyper-competitive domestic markets have driven companies to look further afield in their search for competitive advantage. Although I think the process has really been accelerated by rapid advances in IT and telecoms. That's been the real catalyst for change.

I   And what's the great attraction? Why are companies so keen to source abroad?

C   It depends on the circumstances of the company in question. It could be anything from better access to overseas markets, lower taxes, lower labour costs, quicker delivery or a combination of any of these.

I   But it would be fair to say the financial benefits are the main incentive, wouldn't it?

C   In most cases it probably would, yes. Without them, I suppose few companies would be that interested. But there are risks involved as well, you know.

I   And what are those risks?

C   Well, the most common mistake companies make is they only see the savings and don't bother to think about the effect on other key criteria like quality and delivery. A clothing company that only buys from Asian suppliers at low cost, for instance, will find that as labour rates increase over time, it'll have to island hop to find new low cost sites. And this, of course, introduces uncertainty about quality - and that's critical for a clothing company. There are other possible risks as well.

I   Such as?

C   Well, such as negative publicity as a result of poor working conditions in the supplier's country. And, of course, there's always currency exchange risk.

I   So how do you go about weighing up all these factors and choosing a supplier?

C   It's crucial that companies know precisely what they're after from a supplier and that they fully understand their key selection criteria. They need to be careful to define them and make sure they're measurable and then rank them. It's dangerous selecting a particular supplier just because they happen to deliver outstanding performance in one objective such as cost or flexibility.

I   So, having selected a prospective partner, what then?

C   Well, then you have to negotiate how closely the two parties need to work together. If it's going to be a long-term relationship, you need to discuss how much sharing of information and resources will be necessary to extract maximum value from the collaboration. The prospective partners need to sit down and decide on the best form for the relationship to take.

I   And what's the most common form of this relationship?

C   Well, once again it depends on individual circumstances. The relationship can be anything, I suppose, from complete ownership through strategic alliances to buying the market.

I   Buying the market? What's that?

C   That's when companies just publish their specifications and ask prequalified vendors to bid for the contract. General Electric is currently doing $1bn of business this way over the Internet. It's a short-term deal with almost no interaction with the supplier and the length of the bidding process is cut by half. But most importantly for companies like GE, order processing is $5 an order as opposed to $50 when it's done on paper.

I   You mentioned strategic alliances. When do they make sense?

C   Well, for an aircraft manufacturer like Boeing, for example, an alliance with its engine manufacturers is logical because of the complex interaction between the body of the aircraft and its engines. And this complexity means everything has to be developed together. The arrangement also has the added bonus of reducing the financial risk of long-term development programmes.

I   And how about actually owning the supplier, then? When is that preferable?

C   Well, companies take over suppliers when they're vulnerable to fluctuations in the availability of key supplies. Take Du Pont, for example, the chemicals giant. Since oil is a primary ingredient of many of its products, Du Pont is very much affected by the availability, and therefore cost, of oil. Du Pont reduced these uncertainties by purchasing Conoco, its main oil supplier.

I   Thus keeping its costs down.

C   Possibly. Owning the supplier definitely increases financial control of the supply chain. But when you take the cost of acquisition into account, there are no short-term savings.

I   So, all in all, does global sourcing make sense?

C   Well, there are lots of very powerful benefits but managers have to consider all the main operational factors very carefully first.

Unit 8: Exam practice (Exam focus audio cd)

Listening Test Part One

Good morning. First of all, thank you for inviting me to talk about our electronic meetings system. I've got a handout to give you at the end. But please feel free to make notes.

So, what is DecisionMaker®? Well, quite simply, it enables you to conduct meetings either face-to-face or remotely using networked computers. Now, you're probably wondering 'What's the point of using computers?'. Well, the point is that unlike traditional meetings, everyone gets the chance to contribute because they communicate through the keyboard. This means people can communicate openly with no fear of criticism. And believe me, that can make a big, big difference.

So what are the key advantages of DecisionMaker®? Well, first of all, there is simultaneous input, meaning that everyone 'talks' at once - although electronically, of course. This produces lots of contributions as the process draws on the creative energy of the whole team - not just individuals. Also, because ideas are submitted anonymously, people are free to 'think the unthinkable'. Now this may not sound like much, but believe me, it's a fantastic way of promoting innovation within your company. It also means that all ideas are the property of the team - which is a great boost to team spirit. And each suggestion is evaluated on merit and not on feelings towards the person who came up with it. Imagine that. A meeting without any personal politics.

With DecisionMaker®, ideas belong to the group. This means they are analysed objectively without personal feelings interfering with the way they are developed or rejected. Thus ideas are processed far more quickly than in traditional meetings. And with everyone getting involved at the same level, there is no domination of the proceedings by one or two strong characters. What's more, because the meeting's conducted on computers, everything is automatically recorded so there's no need for a secretary to take notes or minutes. But of course, the real beauty of the system is that you don't need to be in the same place - or even the same country - to hold the meeting!

So, how does it work? Well, let's look at some of the key features of DecisionMaker®. First of all, there's the Whiteboard®, which makes drawings produced during the meeting available to everyone else in the group. Pen passing and free-for-all drawings are also supported. Next we have FileShare®. With this function, the distribution of documents among the team couldn't be easier. Whether it's a spreadsheet, report or graphic image, just drag it into the FileShare window and it's accessible to the team. Thirdly, Consensus® gives instant feedback on suggestions by using one of three voting methods. There's the 10 Point Scale, Yes/No, and Agree/Disagree. Once more, all votes are anonymous so honesty is guaranteed. And finally, there's Briefcase®, which lets you access your favourite applications during the meeting. If you want to use things like your calculator, your calendar or notepad, simply drag them into the Briefcase and they'll be available whenever you need them.

Right, I'd now like to demonstrate just how the system works.

Listening Test Part Two

I'm quite well organised really so I have no problems dealing with things like credit notes and invoices. What I do find stressful, though, is having to deal with people when they ring up and complain about damaged goods or a late delivery. We're only a small company, you know, so it's up to me and my colleague to sort things out. Although, having said that, my colleague isn't actually that big a help at all. She spends most of her day gossiping to friends, so people can only get through to my extension. It's no good trying to interrupt her either. She just shrugs her shoulders and carries on. It's very irritating, you know.

My new colleague's really nice. She worked in Despatch up until about three months ago, so she's already familiar with all the forms and things we use here at the company. I've started her off on some basic procedures, like paying salaries and dealing with credit control, which means that I can concentrate on preparing for next month's audit. She's doing quite well actually - well, when she finally makes it into the office, that is. It's almost 20 past by the time she's gets in ... and even later if she goes to the canteen to get something to eat first. I think she just goes there for a good gossip with her friends from Despatch, myself.

Well, I sometimes struggle to keep my cool with the Sales Department always on at us to get things moving more quickly. We're busy enough as it is, what with planning and organising operations, scheduling projects and dealing with plant maintenance. It doesn't help having to share such a small space with my boss. Well, we get on all right even though he's quite a tidy person and I tend to leave the place in a bit of a mess. But what really does annoy me is the amount of time I have to spend unjamming the printer or the photocopier after he's been using it. I just find it so inconsiderate of him to leave me to deal with it all the time.

I'm used to keeping records of prices and ordering office supplies, of course, but I never realised there would be so much to the job. I mean, when I think back to the interview, the Personnel Manager didn't mention half the things I'm now doing. I've never had to actually select the suppliers myself before. It's a real balancing act, getting the right product at the right price. But my colleague's given me lots of useful information. In fact, there isn't much he hasn't told me. We took a break together on my first day here and he didn't waste any time telling me all about everyone in the office. It makes me wonder now what he's saying behind my back.

It's been a real nightmare lately. We're busy enough at the best of times. And now we've lost our admin assistant, it's even worse. I've been up to my neck in paperwork, going through contract details with the Legal Department and checking CVs and references. You know, I've interviewed 40 applicants this week already for one of our vacancies and it's only Wednesday today. My colleague seems to take everything in his stride, though. If he's not standing next to the fax machine chatting to someone from the Purchasing Department, he's outside my window smoking. Look, there he is, lighting up again. I can't believe it. That's his sixth one this morning. Honestly, it's a wonder he gets any work done at all.

Listening Test Part Three

J = Jim   S= Sally

J   Welcome to Working Hours. In studio today we have Sally Michaels, HR Director at ZSV Insurance, one of many companies promoting flexible working schemes. Hello, Sally.
S   Hello, Jim.
J   So, Sally, what made ZSV decide to move away from the rigid 9-5?
S   Well, social changes have been a major factor. More women are now returning to work after having children, for example. And, even more importantly, we've had to cater for changing customer demands. With customers now preferring to do their business over the phone, we need our staff to work more flexible hours. We also took over two smaller companies recently. So we wanted a common scheme to unite all our new employees.

J   So what are the advantages of the scheme for ZSV?
S   Well, for one thing, we put great emphasis on providing our staff with regular, high quality training. It costs a lot of time and money to train our employees. So, obviously, it makes sense to retain them.
J   And providing them with flexible working patterns can help you do that?
S   That's right. But that isn't the main benefit. We see the scheme as primarily a tool for attracting potential staff to our company - especially high-calibre graduates.
J   Speaking of your staff, what's the main attraction for them?
S   Well, the majority of people in the scheme want to spend more time improving their qualifications by doing an MBA or something like that.
J   I imagine the scheme must make it much easier for staff to look after their children too.
S   Yes, that is an added benefit, as is being able to dedicate more time to their outside interests, such as sports.
J   Now, I believe the scheme isn't totally new.
S   That's right. There was an old scheme but awareness of it was very low. Most men, for example, assumed it was only available to women, which, of course, wasn't the case. The new scheme will also continue to offer alternative working patterns to staff on both short and long-term contracts. Only this time, we're making it available to employees at all levels of the organisation and not just people in more junior positions.
J   I see. And what do you think will be the most popular element of the scheme? Flexible hours?
S   It's difficult to say at the moment but, yes, flexitime is likely to be popular. Typically, though, with the old scheme, employees showed most interest in having longer breaks from work, and I expect it'll be the same this time. There might be some interest in, say, job share arrangements in the future. But we'll have to wait and see.
J   And ZSV is also encouraging teleworking, I believe.
S   Yes, we are.
J   Now, how does that work? Do you use video-conferencing, for example?
S   Well, we have the facilities but they're not that widely used at the moment. As most of our teleworkers have access to the company network, they tend to communicate electronically. It's far more convenient than telephoning because you don't have to worry about whether the person's available or not.
J   That's interesting. But what about your managers, what challenges do they face working from home?
S   Well, several have mentioned the need to be self-disciplined, differentiating between work-time and private time. But the biggest difficulty seems to be empowering others to act for you, especially when they're in the office and you are not.
J   That's surprising. I would have thought the most difficult thing would be staying motivated without the support of colleagues.
S   Well, that's not something that's come up so far but I'm sure it will.
J   So, how do employees get selected as teleworkers?
S   Well, it all begins with an interview with your line manager.
J   To discuss whether the home environment is suitable, you mean?
S   Well, it's not quite as simple as that. The main reason we have the interview is to ascertain whether the applicant's duties are compatible with working from home. It's easier, say, for an IT specialist to work from home than a PA. If the interview goes OK, we then introduce the applicant to a colleague with personal experience of teleworking. We think it's important for the applicant to hear what it's really like working on your own at home.
J   Well, I'm afraid time's running out so we'll have to stop there. Thank you, Sally, for joining us today.

Answer key

Ex ❶:
1	A	2	C	3	C	4	C
5	A	6	B	7	A	8	C

Ex ❷: *Suggested answer:*

1   The company has just set up a new job share system.

2   He was given feedback on his performance during his job appraisal. *2*

3   Her job description didn't outline her main duties and responsibilities very clearly.

4   I'm really enjoying my new job.

5   The employees carried out the job as soon as they were given their brief.

6   WorkSet was used to classify and highlight aspects of the job.

7   One of the most important things in this job is the ability to communicate.

8   We need to monitor the way he carries out his job.

Ex ❸:

2   It was suggested that some training should be/be organised for our team leaders.

3   It was decided that a consultant should be brought in/be brought in/to bring in a consultant.

4   It was found that team leaders' roles are not/were not clear enough.

5   It was agreed that we should start/we start implementing WorkSet the following month.

6   We recommend that Ekstrom should set up/sets up/set up new assessment centres.

Ex ❹:

2   hold
3   says
4   aren't/are not delegating
5   doesn't/does not seem to be getting
6   's/is even bringing
7   think
8   I'm/I am definitely getting

Ex ❶:
2	virtual team	3	corporate intranet
4	line manager	5	business environment
6	hierarchical organisation	7	on-line support
8	operating costs		

Ex ❷:

Verb	Noun	Adjective
standardise	standardisation	standard/standardised
diversify	diversity	diverse/diversified
respond	response/responsiveness	responsive

operate	operation	operating
suit	suitability	suitable
supervise	supervision	supervisory
vary	variety	varied

Ex ❸:
1	remote	2	sequential	3	virtual
4	specify	5	back up	6	interaction
7	challenge	8	impact	9	e-mail
10	motivation				

Ex ❹:
1	into	2	for	3	under
4	on	5	with	6	on

Ex ❺:
1	Correct	2	those	3	such
4	Correct	5	have	6	Correct
7	lot	8	Correct	9	themselves
10	Correct	11	and	12	the

Ex ❻:

2   've/have just promoted
3   hasn't/has not even been working **or** hasn't/has not even worked
4   did she join
5   told
6   saw
7   's/has broken
8   's/has been looking
9   thought
10   was
11   's/has made
12   have already been calling
13   's/has he taken **or** did he take
14   didn't/did not mention

Unit 1:   Exam practice

R1:
1	D	2	C	3	B	4	E
5	A	6	B	7	E	8	C

R5:
1	more	2	from
3	on	4	some/a
5	how	6	the
7	their	8	is
9	such	10	up

Ex ❶:
1	peak	2	level off
3	general upward trend	4	fluctuate
5	bottom out	6	recover

Ex ❷:
1	shares	2	flotation
3	broker	4	investment
5	listings	6	commission
7	merger	8	dividends

Ex ❸:
1	Neutral	2	Positive
3	Negative	4	Positive
5	Negative	6	Negative
7	Positive	8	Neutral

Ex ❹: *Suggested answer:* *(133 words)*

This year, April sales of Fresh 'n' Cool reached 725,000 units, which was slightly down on last year's total. May saw sales fall to a new low of 700,000 units before they began to make a recovery in June. Sales rose steadily to peak at 1.3m units in July. However, in August, they fell slightly, to 1.25m units.

In contrast to this spring's poor performance, last year's sales showed strong growth between April and July, rising from 750,000 to over 1.25m units. However, they then fell sharply in August, finishing back at their April level of 750,000 units.

Therefore, although sales of Fresh 'n' Cool were initially down on last year's figures for the same period, they actually had a much stronger finish this year equalling last year's July peak of 1.25m units.

Ex ❺: **At** *the start of 1996, shares in Consort Industries stood at $160. However, by the end of the year they* **had collapsed** *to just $50. They recovered* **steadily** *over the next twelve months but* **fluctuated** *sharply all through 1998. In 1999 they continued their* **recovery, climbing** *to $160 per share, where they remained throughout 2000.*

Shares in Mandarin Technologies started trading at $150. Like Consort, Mandarin saw **its** *shares fall during 1996 and then* **pick up** *the following year. This recovery then* **turned** *into a general upward trend,* **which** *continued until late 1999, when shares peaked at $220. They then collapsed before* **rising** *briefly to just over $150 at the end of 2000.*

Unit 2b: Mergers & acquisitions (Self-study)

Ex ❶:

Acquired another company	Merged with another company	Was acquired by another company
AT&T	Astra	Bankers Trust
BMW	Chrysler	Matra
Deutsche Bank	Daimler	Media One
Siemens	Exxon	Rover
Vodafone	Mobil	
	Zeneca	

the year of	the merger
	our first international product launch
	increased merger activity
the accelerated rate of	globalisation
	growth
	expansion
the record performance of	stock markets
	shares
	sales
the strength of	their inflated share prices
	the market
	the euro against the dollar
the arrival of	the single European currency
	their new product on the market
	technological innovations

the result of	global economic trends
	the merger
	these job losses
the coming together of	different corporate cultures
	two companies
	both parties
the challenge of	integrating two very different corporate and national cultures
	restructuring the department
	increasing profit margins
the prospect of	redundancies
	failure
	leaving

Ex ❷:

1	takeover	2	merging
3	growth	4	competitive
5	benefits	6	streamline
7	restructuring	8	acquisition

Ex ❸:

2 integrate different cultures
3 add long-term value
4 undercut competitors' prices
5 reduce operating costs
6 generate cost improvements

Ex ❹:

1	to	2	represents/is
3	that	4	its
5	whether	6	not
7	while	8	such

Ex ❺: *The merger raises a number of HR issues (1)* **which/that** *will need to be addressed as a matter of urgency and in a manner (2)* **which/that** *is seen to be fair to the employees of both companies. Firstly, the pay structures of the two companies, (3)* **which** *show marked differences, will need to be reviewed and harmonised. Furthermore, redundancy terms will have to be agreed and offered to employees (4)* **who/that** *lose their jobs as a result of the merger. This is particularly important with regard to senior managers (5)* **whose** *contracts contain severance clauses (6)* **which/that** *guarantee them generous terms. Our approach to these job cuts, (7)* **which** *were promised to shareholders as part of the terms of the merger, will also have a major effect on staff morale within the newly-formed company. It is imperative that we avoid any deterioration of staff morale, (8)* **which** *could have an adverse effect on company performance.*

NB: If **which** *or* **who** *can be replaced by* **that**, *no comma is used.*

Unit 2:   Exam practice

R2:

1	D	2	C	3	E
4	F	5	G	6	A

R4:

1	C	2	B	3	A	4	C
5	D	6	C	7	A	8	D
9	B	10	B				

R5:

1 had	2 what	3 as
4 out	5 many	6 such
7 no	8 all	9 which
10 their		

R6A:

1 order	2 a	3 been
4 Correct	5 which	6 Correct
7 in	8 the	9 but
10 Correct	11 be	12 you

R6B:

1 they	2 Correct	3 Correct
4 have	5 Correct	6 that
7 of	8 Correct	9 to
10 a	11 make	12 for

Unit 3a: Trade fairs (Self-study)

Ex ❶:

1 a	2 Correct
3 do	4 Correct
5 which	6 Correct
7 it	8 these
9 Correct	10 and
11 Correct	12 are

Ex ❷:

1 advertisement
2 reply
3 application
4 design
5 events
6 benefits
7 stands
8 retailers
9 brochures

Ex ❸:
2 With reference to your letter of
3 We look forward to meeting you
4 Further to our conversation of
5 Should you have any further questions
6 Please do not hesitate to contact me

Ex ❹:
2 lands
3 get
4 arrive
5 will take/is going to take/is taking
6 have checked in
7 get
8 go

Unit 3b: Entering a market (Self-study)

Ex ❶:
purposes
trip
association
practices
norms
card
acquaintance

Ex ❷:

1 invest in	2 intend to
3 amount to	4 build on
5 allow for	6 participate in
7 respond to	8 enquire about

Ex ❸:

make	do	enter into
conversation	a mailshot	a joint venture
an investment	business	a partnership
a request	research	a relationship
a commitment	preparatory work	

Ex ❹: *Suggested answer:*   *(130 words)*

Doing business in London and Beijing

Looking at the overall situation, it is far cheaper to do business in Beijing than in London. The most dramatic differences can be seen in the cost of office space and salaries. Renting office space is currently ten times cheaper in Beijing than in London. Likewise, a bilingual secretary in Beijing earns barely a tenth of the going rate in London. The cost of a local phone call in China is more reasonable than in the United Kingdom, a five-minute call being approximately 25% cheaper in Beijing, as is the average cost of accommodation at a five-star hotel. The single area in which Beijing outstrips London in terms of cost is rent, with the price almost double that of a comparable property in London.

Ex ❺:
2 forge relationships
3 pledge investment
4 produce trade literature
5 swap business cards
6 provide hospitality
7 start proceedings
8 match needs

Ex ❻: At meetings with **the** Chinese, **the** leader of your group will be expected to enter first and will generally be offered **a** seat beside **the** most senior Chinese person present. This person will usually chair **the** meeting and act as **the/---** host. At **the** beginning of **the** meeting, all **the** people present will greet each other and swap business cards, after which **a** period of small talk begins. **The** host will then officially start **the/---** proceedings with **a** brief introduction to **the** Chinese enterprise. **The** visiting team is then invited to speak. It is appropriate at this point for foreign participants to make their case and answer questions. Following **the** meeting **the** Chinese enterprise will probably arrange **a** special dinner for **the** overseas guests along with other entertainment such as sightseeing. Guests should always accept these invitations as small talk in **a** social setting is essential for forging relationships with **the** Chinese.

Unit 3:   Exam practice

R3:

1 B	2 C
3 D	4 D
5 B	6 A

Suggested answer: *(229 words)*

Dear Mr Salter

Re: Reference for Mr John Bridge

Further to your letter dated 15 October, I am writing concerning the application of John Bridge for the position of Training Manager at STC International.

I have known John for over 15 years, and feel that the length of our friendship, together with my personal experience of working as Training Manager at Tarbus UK, allows me to comment on his suitability for the advertised position.

As you are aware, John is currently employed by Tarbus UK as Training Co-ordinator for the busy Marmouth branch, where his main responsibility is to assess the training needs of the employees and arrange training programmes to meet these needs. This involves liaising with a large number of language and business skills organisations as well as evaluating the effectiveness of the training employees receive.

John has excellent interpersonal skills and is sociable, patient and a good listener. As a friend, I particularly appreciate his loyalty and sense of humour. I also admire the calm and logical way in which he approaches difficult situations.

I have no hesitation in recommending him for the position of Training Manager for your company and wish him every success in his application.

If you have any further questions, please do not hesitate to contact me, either at the above address or on (01420) 655567.

Yours sincerely

Julia Shipton
Training Manager

Unit 4a: The future of work (Self-study)

Ex ❶: 1 *Negative*   2 *Positive*   3 *Negative*
4 *Negative*   5 *Positive*   6 *Positive*

Ex ❷: 1 *C*   2 *A*   3 *B*
4 *A*   5 *B*   6 *A*
7 *B*   8 *C*

Ex ❸: 2 *foster team spirit*
3 *key a number into a telephone terminal*
4 *run out of supplies*
5 *show interest*
6 *centralise operations*
7 *adapt to a new way of working*
8 *vacate premises*

Ex ❹: 1 *between*   2 *on*   3 *on*
4 *to*   5 *into*   6 *on*

Ex ❺: *meet needs, spend time, run a meeting, predict needs, suit needs, hold a meeting, waste time*

Ex ❻: 2 *It is unlikely that the office will cease to be important.*

3 *The Internet looks set to explode.*

4 *More people are bound to want to work from home.*

5 *It is improbable that everyone will want Internet access.*

6 *Working from home will undoubtedly increase in future.*

Unit 4b: e-business (Self-study)

Ex ❶: 1 *no/little*   2 *their*   3 *that/how*   4 *but*
5 *such*   6 *the*   7 *any*   8 *which/that*

Ex ❷:

1	i	n	t	e	r	n	e	t			
	2	w	e	b	s	i	t	e			
		3	b	u	l	l	e	t	i	n	s
4	t	r	a	n	s	a	c	t	i	o	n	s
		5	o	n	l	i	n	e			
			6	i	n	t	r	a	n	e	t
	7	i	n	t	e	g	r	a	t	e	
8	b	r	o	w	s	e	r				
		9	c	u	s	t	o	m	e	r	s

Ex ❸: 2 *manage inventories*
3 *improve operating efficiencies*
4 *handle transactions*
5 *communicate with partners*
6 *analyse customer behaviour*
7 *personalise offerings*
8 *anticipate customer wants*

Ex ❹: 2 *after-sales service*
3 *product support*
4 *staff turnover*
5 *customer base*
6 *distance learning*

Ex ❺: *Suggested answer:*

2 *We'll be doing more on-line training in future.*

3 *She won't have finished the report by the end of next week.*

4 *We won't be using any paper invoices next year.*

5 *He will have completed the website by July.*

6 *I'll be rethinking our Internet strategy over the next few weeks.*

7 *Internet usage will have doubled within 5 years.*

8 *We won't be launching the products until the website has been completed.*

Unit 4: Exam practice

L1:
1	1975	2	popularity
3	suitable premises	4	rapid expansion
5	substantial contracts	6	resources and knowledge
7	high-street chemist	8	new factory
9	brand name	10	marketing operations
11	family atmosphere	12	market leader

L2:
13 D	14 B	15 C	16 E
17 G	18 N	19 K	20 J
21 L	22 M		

L3:
23 A	24 C	25 B	26 B
27 C	28 A	29 A	30 A

R4:
1 B	2 C	3 D	4 A
5 C	6 A	7 D	8 A
9 B	10 C		

Unit 5a: Staff motivation (Self-study)

Ex ❶:
1	being	2	which
3	Correct	4	Correct
5	such	6	of
7	any	8	Correct
9	those	10	certain
11	Correct	12	the

Ex ❷:
1	ineffective	2	insignificant
3	unsatisfactory	4	irregular
5	unappreciated	6	inflexible
7	irresponsible	8	uninteresting
9	incapable	10	unspecific

1	unappreciated	2	incapable
3	interesting	4	specific
5	irregular	6	ineffective
7	inflexible	8	irresponsible

Ex ❸:
2	restore	repair
3	schedule	plan
4	appreciate	value
5	sever	cut
6	rename	rebrand
7	address	deal with
8	quit	resign

Ex ❹:
1	into	2	from	3	towards/to
4	behind	5	of	6	as

Ex ❺:
2 are awarded
3 are not based
4 has been criticised
5 was introduced
6 have been noticed
7 will be/is going to be reviewed
8 are currently being encouraged
9 is also provided/has also been provided
10 can be found

Unit 5b: Recruitment (Self-study)

Ex ❶:
1 The client instructs the headhunter to fill a vacancy.
2 The headhunter identifies possible candidates.
3 The candidates are interviewed by the headhunter.
4 The headhunter provides a shortlist of candidates.
5 Candidates go through the client's selection process.
6 The client appoints one of the candidates.
7 The client pays the headhunter his completion fee.

Ex ❷:
2 extension number
3 future reference
4 executive search
5 neutral location
6 key player
7 sensitive information
8 skills shortage

Ex ❸:
1	on	2	on
3	for	4	into
5	to	6	across
7	in	8	with
9	to		

Ex ❹:
2 present findings
3 shortlist candidates
4 pay a retainer
5 conduct business
6 compile a list

Ex ❺: *Suggested answer:*

1 The recruitment agency claims there is an acute skills shortage in the IT sector.

2 For recruitment purposes we need an up-to-date copy of your CV.

3 Advertising a job vacancy in newspapers is one recruitment method; using an agency is another.

4 If you're looking for a job, why not apply to a recruitment agency?

5 When recruiting new staff, we look for evidence of exceptional past performance.

6 I have shortlisted candidates with the qualities which we know to be necessary from our previous experience of recruitment.

7 Before he was appointed, he had to go through the client's internal recruitment process.

8 Using a headhunter to recruit a new employee can save a company time.

Ex ❻:
Verb	Noun
apply	**application**
appoint	appointment
compare	**comparison**
explain	**explanation**
categorise	category
recruit	**recruitment**

Ex ❼: 2 which 3 its
4 which 5 those
6 which 7 This
8 who/that 9 this/such
10 these/the

Unit 5: Exam practice

R1: 1 B 2 C 3 E 4 A
5 D 6 C 7 B 8 E

R5: 1 which 2 unlike
3 however 4 only
5 each 6 a
7 such 8 both/each
9 one 10 than

Unit 6a: Corporate culture (Self-study)

Ex ❶: 1 A 2 A 3 B 4 C
5 C 6 B 7 A 8 A

Ex ❷: 1 adaptations 2 competitors
3 operations 4 promotional
5 interpretations 6 expansion
7 influential 8 perceptive

Ex ❸: 2 similar alike
3 informal casual
4 fresh new
5 economical thrifty
6 vital crucial
7 tough hard
8 global worldwide

Ex ❹: 2 arriving 3 operating
4 restructuring 5 working
6 (to) increase 7 realising
8 to be 9 to let
10 believe 11 confronting
12 to turn 13 to reflect
14 looking 15 modernising
16 to be

Unit 6b: Cultural diversity (Self-study)

Ex ❶: 1 means that 2 However
3 while 4 therefore
5 as opposed to 6 although/while
7 Similarly

Ex ❷: *Suggested answer:* *(133 words)*

Mustermann AG and Svensson AB
The graph shows the changing number of employees at Mustermann and Svensson from 1996 to 2000. Looking at the general trend, there has been an upward movement in the number of employees at Svensson whereas Mustermann has seen numbers fall

dramatically over the same period.

During 1996 and 1997 there were 175,000 employees at Svensson. Employee numbers rose steadily over the following three years to reach 210,000 in 2000.

On the other hand, from 1996 to 1999 Mustermann saw employee numbers fall from 230,000 to an all-time low of below 175,000. In 2000, however, Mustermann felt sufficiently confident to start taking on new employees once more with the result that by the end of the year employee levels stood at 185,000, slightly higher than the figure for 1998.

Ex ❸: 2 fix salary levels
3 conduct a meeting
4 appreciate differences
5 build understanding
6 solve a dilemma
7 follow a strategy
8 hold a belief

Ex ❹:

Verb	Noun
choose	**choice**
succeed	success
expect	**expectation**
affect	effect
pay	**pay/payment**
believe	**belief**
solve	solution
promote	**promotion**
diversify	diversity
examine	**examination**
preserve	preservation

Ex ❺: 2 We needn't have gone there.
3 We shouldn't have adapted the product.
4 We ought to be getting back.
5 The language problems can't have helped.
6 They might be having trouble working together.

Unit 6: Exam practice

R3: 1 A 2 C 3 C
4 D 5 B 6 B

W2A: *Suggested answer:* *(226 words)*

Report: Cost-cutting: Administration Department

Introduction
The aim of this report is to examine ways of cutting costs in the Administration Department and explain the implications of these cuts for the running of the department. It is based on the results of a detailed questionnaire sent to all employees.

Findings
It is clear that within the department there are a number of areas where cost-cutting measures could be taken. The most significant areas of concern are the following:

● *paper*
● *refreshments.*

Recommendations

In order to deal with the issue of paper, it is suggested that the department installs a system to recycle all used printing and photocopying paper. It is expected that by adopting new recycling procedures, the department could save as much as £100 a month.

As for refreshments, it is recommended that tea and coffee should only be offered free to employees during morning and afternoon breaks. At all other times employees should be required to pay for refreshments. This measure should reduce the company's monthly bill for refreshments from £320 to £110, thereby making a saving of over £200.

Conclusion

It is felt that the above measures will result in immediate and substantial savings for the Administration Department. Although these recommendations are not expected to affect the running of the department in any significant way, managers should be prepared to encounter initial resistance from staff.

R4:

1	D	2	C	3	C	4	A
5	A	6	B	7	B	8	A
9	B	10	D				

R5:

1	is	2	although/while
3	with	4	what
5	not	6	for
7	both/all	8	the
9	as	10	few

W2B: *Suggested answer:* (247 words)

Dear Mr Schommartz

Re: Work placement at Shiptols UK,
1 Feb 2000 – 31 July 2000

Further to your appointment as Trainee Public Relations Assistant, I would like to welcome you to Shiptols UK. I would also like to take this opportunity to provide you with some introductory information, both about the company itself and the duties you will be expected to perform during your time here. I trust you will find the following points useful.

Unlike many of our overseas subsidiaries, Shiptols UK is divided into seven main departments: Production, Research and Development, Finance, Personnel, Sales, Marketing and Public Relations. I work in the Public Relations department, which is headed by Jenny Holloway. Public Relations is the smallest department in the company, consisting of fifteen employees, who usually work in teams of five. As my assistant, you will generally report directly to me.

My job mainly involves communicating with our local distributors. However, I am currently in charge of organising a major press launch for our new 'Easywash' washing powder, which is due to take place on 15 April. Initially you will be working with Claire O'Reilly, who is responsible for designing the information packs for the press launch. Your duties will include helping to write articles for the pack and choosing photographs for inclusion.

I look forward to working with you in the near future. In the meantime, if you have any further questions, please contact me on (+44) 1431 23776.

Yours sincerely

Martin Wallis
Communications Officer

Unit 7a: Industrial espionage (Self-study)

Ex ❶: *Examples of industrial espionage:*
infiltrate a competitor, bug an office, hack into a network, leak sensitive information, steal confidential data, resort to shady practices

Measures against industrial espionage:
monitor photocopier use, shred important documents, bring in a security adviser, identify a perpetrator, protect a computer system, install passwords

Ex ❷:

1	this	2	Correct	3	of
4	been	5	to	6	Correct
7	Correct	8	who	9	Correct
10	by	11	it	12	a

Ex ❸:

Verb	Noun	Adjective
accept	acceptance/acceptability	acceptable
suspect	suspect/suspicion	suspect/ suspicious
imitate	imitation	imitation
access	access/accessibility	accessible
analyse	analysis	analytical
secure	security	secure
protect	protection	protective
copy	copy	copiable/copied
identify	identity/identification	identifiable
confuse	confusion	confused/ confusing
isolate	isolation	isolated
break	breakage/breach	broken
measure	measure/measurement	measurable

Ex ❹:

2 call the police
3 bear a grudge
4 devise a system
5 break the law
6 suspect foul play
7 shred paperwork
8 take measures

Ex ❺: *Suggested answer:*

3 're/are
4 can go
5 's/is
6 'd be/would be
7 could also look
8 can give
9 like
10 doesn't have/does not have

11 do you still want
12 didn't find/did not find
13 doesn't/does not need to
14 's/has
15 's found/has found
16 'll put

Unit 7b: Business ethics (Self-study)

Ex ❶: *workplace safety, sexual harassment, racial discrimination, conflict of interest, environmental issues, product safety, competitive practices, privacy, executive salaries, gifts and entertainment/corporate gift-giving, corporate philanthropy, whistle-blowing, legal compliance, fair employment practices, delivery of high quality goods and services, industrial espionage, financial mismanagement*

2	sexual harassment	3	workplace safety
4	legal compliance	5	executive salaries
6	corporate gift-giving	7	racial discrimination
8	whistle-blowing		

Ex ❷:

1	illegal	2	unethical
3	unfair	4	unlawful
5	incorrect	6	unofficial

Ex ❸:

2	measure	precaution
3	conduct	behaviour
4	rule	regulation
5	threat	warning
6	rival	competitor
7	freebie	gift

Ex ❹:

1	who	2	to
3	more	4	did
5	when	6	on
7	that	8	as
9	else	10	a
11	when	12	'd/had

Ex ❺: *Suggested answer:*

2 The boss would have sacked him by now if he weren't the Managing Director's nephew.

3 If we hadn't got that contract, the company wouldn't have survived the recession last year.

4 I'm sure she would have been dismissed if anyone had found out how she was getting her information.

5 If she hadn't been filmed shredding the files, she'd still be working here today.

6 The problem would have been solved more quickly if the company had brought in a consultant earlier.

7 The company wouldn't have known if the new assistant hadn't blown the whistle to the press.

8 If he'd left sooner than he did, the company wouldn't be having all the bad publicity it is right now.

Unit 7: Exam practice

R2:

1	C	2	E	3	A
4	G	5	D	6	B

R6:

1	Correct	2	the	3	which
4	with	5	Correct	6	and
7	that	8	what	9	Correct
10	you	11	Correct	12	a

W2: *Suggested answer:* (240 words)

Report

Working conditions

Introduction
The aim of this report is to assess the main reasons for staff complaints about working conditions and propose ways of improving the situation. It is based on the results of a detailed questionnaire sent to all employees in addition to in-depth interviews with managers and union representatives.

Findings
As might have been expected, low pay is the main reason for staff complaints. Furthermore, a significant number of employees are not satisfied with the current level of bonus payments and fringe benefits. Another major complaint is the employees' working environment. In particular, poor ventilation and lighting in communal areas such as the canteen and coffee room have been highlighted.

Recommendations
In order to deal with the issue of pay, it is recommended that a meeting should be arranged with union representatives to discuss both a review of pay levels and the launch of a range of incentive schemes. This could, for example, lead to the introduction of performance related top-ups, with bonuses being awarded to those employees who exceed a target level of performance per week. In addition, employees who have been with the company for over two years could be entitled to a range of fringe benefits, such as subsidised private health care arrangements. It is also suggested that employees are offered an opportunity to express their views on improving their working environment by using a Suggestions Box, which could be put in the canteen.

Unit 8a: Global brands (Self-study)

Ex ❶:

1	cultural	2	advertising
3	globalise	4	adapts
5	production	6	universally
7	diverse	8	profitably

Ex ❷:

1	with	2	towards
3	with	4	to
5	round/around/on	6	as
7	from		

Ex ❸:

2	busy	hurried
3	essential	vital
4	domestic	national
5	cosmopolitan	diverse
6	robust	strong
7	classic	traditional
8	beneficial	advantageous

Ex ❹: *Suggested answer:* *(139 words)*

Report: Comparison of Microsoft Corporation and Apple Computer, Inc. shares

At the start of the period Microsoft's share price was virtually twice that of Apple, by late November however, Apple had outstripped Microsoft with a share value of almost $100, $10 more than Microsoft.

Microsoft saw its share prices change constantly; they reached a peak of $100 in mid-July, fell to under $80 in mid-August and then recovered to $90 by September. The share price then fluctuated at or around this level until the end of November.

Apple shares, on the other hand, showed an overall upward trend. The price rose from $45 per share in July to almost $80 by mid-September. Following a sharp fall at the beginning of October, the share price picked up and increased steadily, reaching a peak of $100 by the end of November.

Ex ❺:
2 spending power
3 target market
4 global presence
5 creative concept
6 marketing campaign

Ex ❻:
2 Rarely are our advertisements translated.

3 Never before has it been easier to advertise globally.

4 On no account should cultural differences be ignored.

5 Only in Europe have we had any success with it.

6 Under no circumstances should we change the logo.

Unit 8b: Global sourcing (Self-study)

Ex ❶:

1	B	2	C	3	B	4	A
5	B	6	C	7	B	8	B
9	A	10	C				

Ex ❷:

1	No	2	No	3	No	4	Yes
5	Yes	6	No	7	Yes	8	No

Ex ❸:

2	warranty	guarantee
3	attraction	incentive
4	reputation	image
5	plant	machinery
6	premises	buildings

Ex ❹: *Suggested answer:* *(137 words)*

Unemployment in Italy and Germany, 1993 to 1998

General trend
Unemployment figures in both Italy and Germany rose significantly over the period from 1993 to 1998.

Italy
Despite an overall increase, the unemployment figures were characterised by number of peaks and troughs over the six years. In 1993 unemployment stood at just over 9% of the total workforce, rising to 12% in 1995. It then fluctuated around this level until 1998, never falling below 11.5%.

Germany
In contrast, unemployment in Germany rose steadily with far fewer fluctuations, increasing from 8.5% to almost 10% by late 1993. Despite an improvement the following year, with the level falling to just under 9.25%, the upward trend continued, with unemployment reaching a peak of 11.5% by the end of 1997. However, 1998 saw unemployment drop sharply to 10.7% before levelling off.

Ex ❺:
1 were confirmed
2 its
3 the
4 to win
5 who
6 had been holding out
7 had taken place
8 would have created
9 will not be releasing
10 are likely to
11 have also been circulating
12 announced
13 would be
14 are cutbacks feared
15 are made

Unit 8: Exam practice

L1:

1	networked computers	2	fear of criticism
3	creative energy	4	innovation
5	on merit	6	analysed objectively
7	no domination	8	secretary
9	drawings	10	distribution of documents
11	voting methods	12	favourite applications

L2:

13 E	14 C	15 G	16 D
17 H	18 J	19 L	20 P
21 O	22 M		

L3:

23 B	24 B	25 C	26 B
27 C	28 A	29 A	30 B

R4:

1	C	2	D	3	B	4	C
5	A	6	A	7	D	8	C
9	D	10	B				